OVERVIEW

Overview

Some people think that those who present successfully possess a special gift or flair that others do not have. This is not true.

Successful presenters are made, not born. They have all learned good presentation skills and techniques and then honed them through practice. You can do the same.

This book explains that, though there are different basic types of presentation, every presentation you make involves four important components:
- the skill of the presenter,
- your audience,
- the venue,
- your message.

In this book, you will discover how these four elements must interact to produce a presentation that you can be proud of.

You will also find out how to:
- meet the needs of the audience and venue,
- prepare and structure your presentation,

- conquer your nerves.

As with anything else, presentations are built from the bottom up. This book will give you a solid foundation of knowledge and skills, so that you can plan and construct presentations that get your messages across successfully.

You have a presentation to give. You have prepared and rehearsed it. Great. But when you stand up in front of your audience members, they're interested in your delivery, not your preparation.

The challenge now is to powerfully deliver your presentation so that you do justice to your message and yourself.

This book is about getting your message across as well as you possibly can, and the techniques you need to do that.

In essence, good presentation delivery requires three things. You need to:
- create a good first impression,
- hold the audience's attention from start to finish,
- ensure that the presentation is memorable.

Jill is an experienced presenter who knows exactly what she needs to do to successfully deliver her presentation.

Create a good impression

"It's important that the first impression I make on my audience members is a positive one because their first impression will shape their view of me and their receptiveness to my presentation."

Hold the audience's attention

"I put a lot of time into preparing my presentation, so it's important to me that I deliver it in a way that holds the audience members, and keeps them concentrating on what I have to say, from start to finish."

Ensure the presentation is memorable

"My presentation needs to be memorable. I want the audience members to remember what I've said to them, and I want them to remember me as well."

Delivering your presentation in a way that does justice to your message can seem daunting, but it's not. This book teaches you the simple techniques you need to look, and sound, good from the moment you begin speaking.

You'll learn how to hold your audience's attention, and how to make sure your presentation stands out from the crowd so that people remember it.

The thought of speaking in public is a frightening prospect for many people--it seems like a lonely situation. But of book, this is absolutely not true. When you speak in public, you are not alone. You can call on powerful resources. And you should be prepared to do so.

Colleen frequently gives presentations. Experience has taught her that she is never on her own as a presenter, and she has learned to make the most of the resources available to her.

Visual aids

"I often use bright and engaging visual aids. While the audience members are looking at these, it takes the pressure off me."

Questions

"I get the audience members to help me--I ask them questions, and they ask me questions."

Teams

"Sometimes I make a presentation with a team. In that case, I'm directly supported by my colleagues at every stage of the presentation."

Most presentations benefit from visual aids. There are several versatile forms of visual support available to you that will enrich your presentation if you know how to use them appropriately. On most speaking occasions, you should encourage questions; your presentation will be more enjoyable and effective if you do this. Many people enjoy presenting as part of a team. They enjoy both the challenge and the support.

Visual aids, questions, team presentations--knowing when to use these resources and how to use them with flair is the focus of this book.

CHAPTER 1 - PRESENTING SUCCESSFULLY

CHAPTER 1 - Presenting Successfully
  SECTION 1 - Presentation Basics
  SECTION 2 - Preparing Your Presentation
  SECTION 3 - Controlling Yourself and Your Environment

SECTION 1 - PRESENTATION BASICS

SECTION 1 - Presentation Basics

Being a good presenter is not a mysterious process. If you learn the basics and put them into practice, you can be confident of success. Have you ever sat during a presentation and wondered: "What am I supposed to get out of this?"

If you have, it's probably because the speaker isn't clear about the type of presentation that he or she is giving. Every presentation is unique, but will fall into one of a few basic categories. When you're making a presentation, you must be clear about what type of presentation it is.

Have you ever considered what it is that makes an audience respond positively to one speaker, while another speaker of equal ability really struggles? It is not complicated. All successful presenters demonstrate the same qualities, which are not present in unsuccessful presenters.

Have you ever attended a presentation that is interesting, but goes on for too long, so that you lose concentration? There are three external factors that affect

audience concentration. You should take these into account when planning the length of your presentation. These factors are:
- the size of the venue and audience,
- how well equipped the venue is,
- the time of day.

THE BASICS OF PRESENTING

The basics of presenting

Being a good presenter is not a mysterious process. If you learn the basics and put them into practice, you can be confident of success.

John seems to have a head start when it comes to presenting. He's outgoing, and enjoys being the center of attention. He's articulate, and is very experienced since he never turns down a chance to make a presentation. But what does Tom, his colleague, really think of John's presenting skills?

Confused

"Is he talking for my benefit, or just entertaining himself? Sometimes, I don't know what he's inferring."

Frustrated

"I've got better things to do with my time than to listen to somebody tell me stuff that I already know."

John has some natural advantages, but is not capitalizing on them. He needs to show some respect for his audience by learning the fundamentals of presenting. The next time that he gives a presentation, John needs to

Giving Successful Presentations

inform himself properly about the audience and venue, and work on his message. He also needs to remind himself of the qualities of good presenters.

Audience

You will be able to adapt your message and your delivery to audience needs.

Venue

You will be able to make the best possible use of the presentation venue.

Message

You will be able to structure your message so that it is audience-friendly.

Technique

You will be able to communicate your message in a way that encourages the audience to retain it once the presentation is over.

Question

John knows that his presentations could be better. You think that he needs to concentrate on the basics. What do you say to convince him about the benefits of this?

Options:

1. "You will be able to adapt your delivery and your message to your audience."

2. "You will deliver your presentation in an entertaining way."

3. "Your message will be more 'listener-friendly.'"

4. "You will take the location of the presentation into account."

5. "You can be more confident that your message will be remembered."

6. "Your message will tell the audience what they want to hear."

Answer:

Actually, if you get the basics right, you can adapt your delivery and message to the audience and venue, make your presentation audience-friendly, and deliver it so that it is remembered.

Option 1: This is a correct choice. By knowing your audience, you can tailor what you say and how you say it to best serve them. John needs to make sure he doesn't alienate or bore his audience with content they already know.

Option 2: This is an incorrect choice. John already delivers in an entertaining way, but that can obscure the message. His message to the audience may be unclear if he's too entertaining. John should tailor his presentation to the context.

Option 3: This is a correct choice. By being informed about the audience and venue, John can appropriately tailor his presentation to the audience. This makes his presentation more listener-friendly.

Option 4: This choice is correct. For John to be informed prior to a presentation, he needs to look at the venue for the presentation. This will help him prepare better for the particular venue and best use its facilities.

Option 5: This choice is correct. When John understands who he's presenting to and what he needs to present, he can then develop a solid technique for delivery. That technique will help people recall the content better.

Option 6: This choice is incorrect. What the audience wants to hear and what they need to hear are two different things. By informing himself, John can determine what the audience needs to hear and then deliver it in a listener-friendly way.

Remember, whether you are a novice or have years of presenting experience, the same rules apply. Practice makes perfect, but learn the basics first, so that you don't entrench bad habits.

FIVE HYPOTHETICAL AUDIENCES

Five hypothetical audiences

Have you ever sat during a presentation and wondered: "What am I supposed to get out of this?"

If you have, it's probably because the speaker isn't clear about the type of presentation that he or she is giving. Every presentation is unique, but will fall into one of a few basic categories. When you're making a presentation, you must be clear about what type of presentation it is.

Henry: When I'm making a presentation, I'm usually trying to change my listeners' minds, or persuade them to do something.

Amy: That's a common type of presentation for me, too. But don't you also make presentations to inform people of something?

Henry: Sure--that's the other main type of presentation that I give.

Henry and Amy talked about two main types of presentations. In total, there are five basic types. Presentations can be created to:

- motivate,

Giving Successful Presentations

- inform,
- persuade,
- promote discussion,
- entertain.

Think about your own recent presentations. What are the most common types that you use? Are there any types that you never use?

Question

A new colleague, fresh out of college, asks you about the common types of presentations. These types arise from various situations. What are these situations?

Options:

1. when you need to communicate information
2. when you need to brainstorm ideas
3. when you need to persuade or convince people
4. when you need to entertain people
5. when a group needs to discuss an idea or proposal
6. when you need to motivate people

Answer:

People make presentations to inform, motivate, or persuade, and to promote discussion. Occasionally, entertainment is the only reason for a presentation. A brainstorming session is not a presentation.

Option 1: This is a correct choice. One reason to give a presentation may be to provide information to the audience. In this case, you will want to present the information in a logical order.

Option 2: This choice is incorrect. A presentation is not an appropriate venue for brainstorming. A presentation may, however, be for discussion purposes, in which case you would present options and take audience views and questions.

Option 3: This choice is correct. A presentation may be necessary for selling people on the benefits of something--be it a product, process, or idea. Such a presentation would highlight benefits with supporting facts and arguments.

Option 4: This is a correct choice. You may need to give a presentation that is entertaining. In this case, stories and knowledge about the audience will be helpful.

Option 5: This is a correct choice. There may be a need for a presentation that facilitates discussion. To do so, you should present information and options then invite views and questions from the audience.

Option 6: This choice is correct. A presentation may be necessary for motivating people. In such a presentation, you would acknowledge any negative feelings but focus on the future in an upbeat way.

Each of the five types of presentations demands a different approach. Sandrine is a highly experienced presenter. Her approach varies from presentation to presentation.

Motivation

To motivate, Sandrine acknowledges her audience's negative feelings, and then communicates a vision of the future in a positive, upbeat way.

Information

To inform, Sandrine always sequences the information in a logical order, and also asks questions to check audience understanding.

Persuasion

To persuade, Sandrine sells the benefits of the proposal, supports the benefits with facts and arguments, and shows appreciation of the audience's point of view.

Giving Successful Presentations

Discussion

To promote discussion, Sandrine presents a set of options, listens to the audience's views, and answers audience questions.

Entertainment

To entertain, Sandrine tells the audience amusing anecdotes, based on her own experience if possible, or what she knows about her audience. She avoids telling jokes.

Question

Karen has been told to make five different presentations. Her boss, Sita, has left notes about how she should approach each one. Help Karen out by matching each presentation type to the appropriate notes.

Options:

A. persuasion
B. information
C. motivation
D. entertainment
E. discussion

Targets:

1. Use anecdotes based on your own experience.

2. Present the options, then listen to what the audience has to say.

3. Present the benefits, and back them up with facts and arguments.

4. Acknowledge how the audience feels, and communicate your vision in a positive way.

5. Follow a logical, sequential order, and check understanding.

Answer:

Remember to use benefits to persuade, motivate by communicating a vision, present information logically, entertain through anecdotes, and present options and listen to promote discussion.

Anecdotes and other similar strategies are entertaining forms of presentation. By using stories or anecdotes, Karen is giving an entertainment presentation.

When the audience is involved in the conversation about the content, this is a presentation focused on discussion. To facilitate good discussion, they need information, options, and opportunities to speak and ask questions.

When people need to be persuaded, Karen will need to list the benefits. Those benefits have to be supported by facts and arguments; otherwise, the audience will not be persuaded.

When people are lacking motivation, it is often because they have negative feelings about something. A motivational presentation would acknowledge those feelings and refocus on the positive.

Sometimes Karen will need to give presentations that inform the audience. To best inform them, she will need to present information in a logical order and will want to check periodically to make sure they understand her.

You should vary your approach depending on the style of presentation that you are giving, just as Sandrine does. You also need to know when to use each different presentation style. Miko has asked for Sandrine's help. He's had negative feedback from some presentations, and thinks that he's using the wrong type for each situation.

Information

"I use this type of presentation to present facts that people need to do their jobs better--for example, product information or changes in procedure."

Persuasion

"This is better when a change in behavior or ideas is necessary, and I have to 'sell' the proposal to the audience."

So, when your audience needs facts, an information presentation is the right approach. When you need to convince people to change their points of view, then a persuasive style of presentation is better.

Motivation

A motivational presentation is best when your audience is demoralized by a change, or lacks optimism about--or confidence in--the future. Your job is then to enthuse your listeners.

Discussion

A discussion style works well when you have a decision to make that will affect your audience. You present the options first, and find out people's views, so that you can take their preferences into account.

Entertainment

An entertaining style of presentation is best for when you want people to enjoy themselves by establishing a fun, light-hearted mood. For example, you might want to do this at the end of a conference, or at a part-social, part-business dinner.

Choosing the right presentation style for the occasion, and varying your approach to suit the style, will set you firmly on the path to delivering great presentations.

As chief executive, George has to talk to many different groups at the annual conference. The field sales people don't know enough about the new range of boots. What do his department heads think about the proposed new vacation schedule? The dispatch team leaders can't see why they have to move offices. The telesales people aren't happy about job cuts. And at the closing dinner, George has to send everyone away happy.

Field sales

"I am going to explain all the data that you need to answer customer questions about the boots, and in the order that you are likely to get them. I'll check with you as I proceed, to make sure that I'm being clear."

Department heads

"I have to make decisions this month about the new vacation schedule, which will affect you all. There are several possibilities, and I'd like to hear what you think of them, so that I can add your views to the equation."

Dispatch

"I'm sure that you will all be better off in the new office. It's not only bigger and better equipped, but it's superior in other ways, which I'd like to explain now."

Telesales

"There have been a lot of upheavals in your department this year, I know that. But the process is now complete, and you can look forward to a prosperous and stable future with the company."

Closing dinner

"I want to say a few words before we all disband. No jokes, I promise! But it's time to look back on a few unexpected things that happened during this conference, which could have come from the pages of a novel. And my agent's waiting with bated breath..."

Giving Successful Presentations

George is a very versatile speaker, which is good because each of his five presentations were of a different type.
Field sales
George chooses an information presentation to the field sales people. They have to be able to talk about the product features confidently, and George presents the data in a way that is rational, and will be easy to process.
Department heads
George will have to make the final decision about vacation schedules, but giving a discussion presentation allows him to respond to the legitimate concerns of his senior colleagues.
Dispatch
George wants to convince the people in dispatch that the office move is a good idea. The best way to do this is to give them facts and arguments that explain the benefits.
Telephone sales
The telesales people have had some bad experiences, and their confidence is low. George must acknowledge the negative feelings and then sell his vision of the future.
Conclude
At the end of a difficult conference, nobody wants a speech full of heavy content. George needs to talk about light, humorous topics to send them all home happy.
Question
Presentations are an important part of your job as factory manager at Tasty Pastries. This week alone, you have had to make five presentations. Match each audience type to the most appropriate kind of presentation you could use for them.
Options:

A. technical crew
B. packaging department
C. machinists
D. juniors
E. everyone

Targets:

1. motivation
2. discussion
3. information
4. persuasion
5. entertainment

Answer:

In fact, the technical crew needs information, the packaging people need to be convinced, you need to discuss changes with the machinists, the juniors have to be motivated, and at the party everyone will want to be entertained.

The juniors are in need of motivation. For this group, you will need to acknowledge their negative feelings. Your job is to inspire the juniors and motivate them to move forward.

You must discuss the line layout with the machinists and take their views into account as a result. For this presentation, you will present options and then take audience views and questions.

The technical crew simply needs to know about routine maintenance procedures. For this, you will give an informative presentation that provides information in a logical order.

The people in the packaging department need to be convinced that the change is good. In this instance, you will be giving a persuasive presentation that focuses on benefits with supporting facts and arguments.

When everyone is together at the party, you will want to use an entertaining speech. You should keep it light and use entertaining anecdotes or stories.

The key to deciding on presentation style is to consider your audience's needs. The packaging people have the information, but you need to convince them to change. The juniors don't need straight information either--but they do need to be motivated. You must discuss the line layout with the machinists to take their views into account. Once you've decided on a layout, then you might need to persuade them, but for now, you require their input.

The other two presentations will be easier. The technical crew only requires information about routine maintenance in a logical order. And at the party, people will only be expecting some brief anecdotes. When you have a presentation to make, always be clear in your own mind which of the five styles to choose. That way, you'll be better positioned to meet the needs of your audience.

THE EFFECTIVENESS OF A SPEAKER

The effectiveness of a speaker

Have you ever considered what it is that makes an audience respond positively to one speaker, while another speaker of equal ability really struggles? It is not complicated. All successful presenters demonstrate the same qualities, which are not present in unsuccessful presenters.

If you show your audience these qualities, they will respond positively to you, and engage with your presentation. To make a successful presentation, you need to do the following:
- behave confidently,
- interact with the audience,
- demonstrate the physical skills of presenting.

Joanna was in the audience for Angela's last presentation. Now Angela wants to know if she showed the qualities of a good presenter.

Joanna: I don't know how you felt inside, but you looked confident, without seeming arrogant.

Giving Successful Presentations

Angela: That's good. Do you think that I interacted enough with the audience?

Joanna: Yes--just the right amount. There was interaction between you and us, but not all of the time.

Angela: That's what I was trying to accomplish.

Joanna: Well, you succeeded.

Angela: And do you think that I showed the physical skills of a presenter?

Joanna: I'd say so. You seemed comfortable with the computer that you were using to show your slides.

Demonstrating the basics of a successful presenter means getting the balance right. You want to look confident, but not arrogant. You need interactivity, but too much can disrupt the flow of your presentation. Demonstrating the physical skills of a presenter means looking comfortable with the technology that you use. Show these three qualities, and your audience will concentrate on what you have to say. If you do not demonstrate them, people will become distracted from your message.

Question

Your colleague, Dwayne, is about to make his first presentation. He's pretty sure that all good presenters demonstrate the same basic qualities, but he's not so sure what they are. What do you say to him?

Options:

1. "Make sure that your manager is happy with your subject matter."

2. "You need to have interactivity between yourself and your audience."

3. "It's important to come across as confident."

4. "You must encourage maximum interactivity between yourself and the audience."

5. "Become comfortable with physical presentation methods and technology."

Answer:

In fact, all successful presenters demonstrate confidence, interaction with the audience, and the relevant physical skills.

Option 1: This is an incorrect choice. A manager's approval of the content has nothing to do with being a good presenter. A good presenter is confident, interacts with the audience, and uses the presentation materials well.

Option 2: This is a correct choice. A good presenter interacts with the audience. However, a good presenter is also careful to balance the level of interaction between too little and too much.

Option 3: This choice is correct. A good presenter appears confident with the content and with being in front of an audience. That confidence does not become overbearing to the point of seeming arrogant, which can put off an audience.

Option 4: This is an incorrect choice. A key to all aspects of being a good presenter is balance. With interactivity, balance comes in interacting just enough with the audience. Too much interaction may cause you to lose control of the presentation.

Option 5: This choice is correct. Audience members should observe that you handle the equipment and materials well during your presentation. This means that you don't fumble with the technology or make a lot of mistakes.

Giving Successful Presentations

Now consider your own presentations. Do you think that you come across as confident? Do you interact with your audience? Do you show the physical skills of a presenter?

Max's audiences rate him as an effective presenter, who demonstrates the three successful presenter qualities. But what exactly does Max do to gain this reputation?

Behave confidently

Max behaves confidently by making eye contact with his audience, moving and gesturing in a natural way, and making sure that he talks clearly in his normal voice.

Interact with your audience

Max interacts with his listeners by directing questions at them, and asking for feedback. He also gives them an opportunity to ask him questions.

Demonstrate physical skills

Max demonstrates his physical presenter skills by dealing confidently with the audiovisual technology that he uses during his presentations. He doesn't fumble or make mistakes, which would distract from his message.

Question

Sanjeev wants to learn from Max, so he sits in on one of Max's presentations, and makes notes on what he does to show the qualities of a successful presenter. Match each presentation quality to one or more of Sanjeev's notes.

Options:

A. behave confidently
B. interact with the audience
C. demonstrate the physical skills of presenting

Targets:

1. He gave us the chance to ask questions.
2. He looked at the audience a lot.

3. He'd obviously practiced using his visual aids.
4. Several times he asked the listeners for their opinions.
5. He spoke and moved very naturally.

Answer:

You need to behave confidently by making eye contact, moving naturally, and using a clear voice. Use questions and feedback to interact, and show your physical skills by handling technology with ease.

Giving the audience a chance to ask questions is a way Max interacts with the audience. This allows them to participate in the presentation and provide feedback or determine a helpful direction.

By looking at the audience, Max makes good eye contact with the people present. This strong eye contact makes Max appear confident during his presentations.

Max doesn't fumble or make mistakes when using the technology. This ease of use demonstrates that Max has the physical skills of presenting.

By asking listeners for their questions, Max is engaging the audience in the presentation. He invites the audience to interact with him through their questions, which audience members like.

The way Max carried himself during a presentation conveyed a sense of confidence. By speaking and moving naturally, he showed that he was comfortable presenting but was not overly arrogant in his approach.

When you make a presentation, your listeners expect you to look and sound pleased to be there, and happy to have the chance to talk to them. Demonstrate the three qualities of successful presenters, and you will meet your audiences' expectations.

Giving Successful Presentations

Aleesha really wants to develop the skills of a successful presenter, so whenever she sees good speakers, she tries to learn from them. Yesterday, she was in the audience for an excellent presentation.

Confidence

"The way that she made eye contact with as many people in the audience as possible looked so confident. Also, she walked around the stage as if she owned it, and used gestures appropriately to emphasize each point."

Interactivity

"The interaction was fun. She passed the new packaging around to let us see it close up, and then asked for our opinions. Then she split us up into groups to come up with new box designs, and finally we had to report back to the group."

Physical skills

"She had excellent physical skills. The way that she used her slides and the whiteboard together was ingenious. And when that sound glitch hit, she didn't falter--but worked around it."

The presenter that Aleesha saw was a great role model. She made genuine eye contact with people, and moved confidently. Make sure that you look as many audience members in the eyes as possible. Don't be tempted to simulate eye contact by looking over people's heads.

With so much interaction going on, Aleesha was bound to remain engaged by the presentation. Also, the fact that the speaker was comfortable with her aids meant that there were no unwanted distractions.

Now, decide how successful a presenter James is. James was a confident and interactive presenter, but there is really no excuse for going into a presentation where you need to play music, and not checking that the CD is in good working order!

To be a successful presenter, you need to be confident, to interact with your audience, and to be comfortable using any physical objects and technology required in your presentation. If you demonstrate these three qualities, your audience will respond positively to you.

THE VENUE, AUDIENCE, AND TIME OF DAY

The venue, audience, and time of day

Have you ever attended a presentation that is interesting, but goes on for too long, so that you lose concentration?

There are three external factors that affect audience concentration. You should take these into account when planning the length of your presentation. These factors are:
- the size of the venue and audience,
- how well equipped the venue is,
- the time of day.

If these factors are favorable, you will be able to keep your audience's attention for longer. If they are unfavorable, you will find it hard to maintain audience focus. This is true in all cases, no matter how hard you work as a presenter. Consider your own presentations for a moment. When you plan them, do you take into account the external factors that limit how long your audience can concentrate?

Remember, once people have stopped listening to what you have to say, you are wasting your time--and theirs.

Question

One of your colleagues has asked you how to maintain audience concentration during presentations. What external factors must he take into account?

Options:

1. how hard he works
2. the size of the venue and audience
3. the quality of the visual aids
4. how well equipped the venue is
5. the time of day

Answer:

Actually, no matter how skilled you are at presenting, the size of venue and audience, venue equipment, and time of day all influence the concentration span of your audience.

Option 1: This is an incorrect choice. Factors affecting audience concentration are external factors. Hard work is an internal factor. External factors include the size of the venue and audience, how well equipped the venue is, and time of day.

Option 2: This is a correct choice. For larger venues and audiences, it's easier for people to fall asleep. Audience members may be in the back and have a hard time seeing. This will affect how well and how long they concentrate.

Option 3: This is an incorrect choice. No matter how nice the visuals are, audience members will lost concentration for other reasons. Audience members lose focus because the venue is too big, the venue seating is poor, or if it's a bad time of day.

Giving Successful Presentations

Option 4: This is a correct choice. How well the venue is equipped includes whether it allows for a variety of presentation modes. However, this also includes seating, temperature, and other environmental aspects.

Option 5: This is a correct choice. Time of day can greatly affect audience concentration. Early morning is best. Audiences get hungry just before lunch and may be lethargic afterwards. Many are tired at the end of the day and don't focus well.

How long can you expect your audience to maintain focus? In favorable conditions, people will concentrate fully for fifteen minutes. You may be able to hold them for thirty minutes, but forty-five would be unlikely.

In unfavorable conditions, concentration spans decline.

Wayne is excellent at public speaking, but on this occasion he has not adapted his presentation to take account of the three external factors that limit concentration. Leo and Carla were in the audience.

Leo: What a long presentation!

Carla: Too long!

Leo: You're right. I was way at the back of everybody, so I couldn't see much, anyway. After a while, I just fell asleep. I don't think that he noticed.

Carla: Well, how did he expect us to listen for fifty minutes so late in the day? I mean, this was the fourth presentation that I've sat through!

Under the circumstances, Wayne should have given a much briefer presentation. He was speaking at the end of a long day, after several other speakers, which meant that concentration levels were naturally low. Also, the talk was being held in a large venue, with a large audience. This meant that Leo could not see properly, and so he lost focus.

Sam is a skillful and energetic presenter, but he knows that he can't just talk to an audience for as long as he wants to. He appreciates the external factors that improve or limit concentration span, and takes these into account.

Audience size

"A small audience in an intimate space is better than a large audience in a big auditorium. In a large space, it's easier for people to switch off."

Variety and venue

"Good audiovisual equipment helps concentration span, by introducing variety. Also, think about seating and heating. Hard seats are distracting, overly soft seats too relaxing. If it's too hot, people will get sleepy; too cold, and they'll fidget."

Time

"People concentrate better if the presentation is in the first half of the morning. If it's immediately before lunch, people get hungry and distracted. If it's after lunch, people can become lethargic."

Question

You are concerned about maintaining audience focus in your presentations at Nouvelle Pharmaceuticals. You make a list of conditions that will improve audience concentration. Which items are on your list?

Options:

1. hard seats, so people can't relax
2. talking to a small audience, rather than a big room full of people
3. talking after lunch, so people have had a break
4. good audiovisual equipment

Giving Successful Presentations

5. average room temperature and comfortable seats
6. scheduling the presentation early in the day
Answer:
In fact, you can maximize audience concentration by using an intimate venue that is neither too hot nor too cold, and quality audiovisual equipment, to introduce variety. Giving your presentation early in the day is best.

Option 1: This is an incorrect choice. Actually, hard seats make it harder for people to concentrate because they are uncomfortable. You will want to check for comfortable seats so people aren't hurting while sitting listening to you.

Option 2: This is a correct choice. If the audience is too big, people in the back may have a hard time seeing or hearing and will probably lose concentration faster. You'll want to make sure you have a smaller audience.

Option 3: This is an incorrect choice. People are usually more lethargic after lunch and may be more inclined to lose concentration and fall asleep. You should try to schedule your presentation for the morning hours.

Option 4: Correct. Good use of audiovisual materials maintains interest and focus. Be sure to check whether your venue is well-equipped for this. This alone, however, will not improve concentration if other environmental features are bad.

Option 5: This choice is correct. The venue should be comfortable for the audience. This includes a temperature that is not too hot or too cold and seats that are comfortable, not too hard or too soft.

Option 6: This is a correct choice. Presenting in the early part of the day is best, so you should try to schedule an early presentation. If you present before lunch, people get hungry. After lunch and at the end of the day, people are tired.

No matter how skilled a presenter you are, adverse external factors can turn what could be a successful presentation into a flop. Make sure you always take these factors into account in the planning stage.

SECTION 2 - PREPARING YOUR PRESENTATION

SECTION 2 - Preparing Your Presentation

Everybody has a different idea for preparing for presentations. But do you prepare in the right way? How you prepare for presentations is a lot more important than how much time you spend. Sandra and Olly are extremely conscientious about preparing for their presentations. Unfortunately, they don't know how to be efficient.

You have an upcoming presentation. You need to prepare it. So where do you start? Preparing effectively involves following a specific procedure in a disciplined way. The first thing that you need to do is to identify the objective of the presentation. Ask yourself: "What do I want my presentation to achieve?"

You know what you want to say in your presentation, but how can you make sure you remember it when faced with your audience? It's all in how you organize your notes. Organize them in the right way, and it boosts your confidence. Choose the wrong method, and all of your hard preparation work will have been wasted. Karl decided to learn his presentation by heart. This is not a good idea, because you are likely to forget something important.

EFFICIENT PRESENTATION PREPARATION

Efficient presentation preparation

Everybody has a different idea for preparing for presentations. But do you prepare in the right way? How you prepare for presentations is a lot more important than how much time you spend. Sandra and Olly are extremely conscientious about preparing for their presentations. Unfortunately, they don't know how to be efficient.

Notes and visual aids

"I spend a lot of time organizing notes and visual aids, until I'm sure that I've covered the whole subject."

Writing

"I spend a lot of time writing about everything that I want to say about the subject. I do a lot of cutting and pasting until it reads perfectly to me."

Sandra is trying to write the perfect speech. Olly is trying to cover the whole subject. Neither of them is thinking about the audience while they are preparing. This is not what good preparation is about.

Preparing your presentation efficiently helps you to:
- keep your audience needs in mind,
- save time,
- cover a realistic amount of content.

Good preparation also allows you to show your skills in the best possible light when standing in front of your audience.

Question

Your colleagues at Diligent Finance seem to be very inefficient when it comes to preparing their presentations. What benefits of good preparation can you highlight to convince them to change?

Options:

1. It saves time.
2. It allows people to cover the subject in full detail.
3. It allows people to show their presentation skills.
4. It ensures that audience needs are taken into account.
5. It helps people to choose a realistic amount of content.

Answer:

Preparing properly will save you time. You won't try to deal with more content than you should, and it helps you to keep your audience needs in mind. Consequently, your skills as a presenter will be able to shine.

Option 1: This is a correct choice. By trying to cover too much or create the perfect presentation, they will spend too much time. Good preparation is efficient preparation, which saves time and creates better presentations.

Option 2: This is an incorrect choice. Covering a subject in full detail can be too much detail. Your

Giving Successful Presentations

colleagues should keep audience needs in mind. Good preparation means covering a realistic amount of content.

Option 3: This is a correct choice. Good preparation sheds the best possible light on the presenter's skills. This reflects positively on the presenter and the topic.

Option 4: This choice is correct. Good preparation means considering your audience. This will help your colleagues avoid cramming too much into a presentation, which will also save them more time.

Option 5: This choice is correct. It may be tempting to put too much time and energy into making sure every point is covered. Good preparation means covering only what is realistic and appropriate for the audience.

In this lesson, you will discover that how much time you spend preparing your presentation does not matter. How efficiently you spend the time, preparing the content and notes, is the key.

A MODEL FOR PREPARING CONTENT

A model for preparing content

You have an upcoming presentation. You need to prepare it. So where do you start?

Preparing effectively involves following a specific procedure in a disciplined way. The first thing that you need to do is to identify the objective of the presentation. Ask yourself: "What do I want my presentation to achieve?"

Write the objective on a piece of paper as a single sentence. Keep it visible on your desk as you prepare your presentation. So, the first stage of the preparation process is to clearly identify your objective. The other two steps are to:

- select your presentation content,
- organize your presentation content.

Consider for a moment how you currently prepare your presentations. Some people try to prepare by simply sitting down at their computers and writing what they want to say, cutting and pasting as they go. Others start by creating a set of slides, and deciding on content later. Neither of these approaches is likely to be effective.

Question

You overhear a group of colleagues discussing how they prepare what they want to say in their presentations. They talk about several steps. Which three steps should they follow first?

Options:
1. cut and paste the content
2. decide on the objective
3. create the slides
4. select the content
5. organize the content

Answer:

First, you need to decide on your objective, and then to select and organize your content to meet this objective.

Option 1: This is an incorrect choice. This approach is not likely to be effective because it doesn't center on a particular objective. Your colleagues should decide on the objectives, then select and organize content based on that direction.

Option 2: This is a correct choice. Your colleagues should clearly identify what they want to achieve with the presentation. Without an objective, it may appear to wander or cover too much. Identifying the objective is the first step.

Option 3: This choice is incorrect. The content should be decided before slides are ever created. Creating slides first is not likely to be effective. Your colleagues should determine the objective then select and organize the content.

Option 4: This is a correct choice. The step of selecting content focuses on what should be covered. This will keep your colleagues' presentations from containing too much.

Option 5: This is a correct choice. It is important that the content be organized in a logical manner. Once your colleagues have selected the appropriate content, they can then begin to organize it into a coherent presentation.

Allison is disciplined in her presentation preparation. She has recently made three presentations with different objectives. In each case, she identified the objective by asking herself: "What do I want my presentation to achieve?" She then wrote each of the objectives as a sentence.

Presentation 1

As a result of this presentation, support staff members will have the information that they need to answer three types of customer query.

Presentation 2

As a result of this presentation, morale in the department will be improved.

Presentation 3

As a result of this presentation, the client will be persuaded to purchase our new product line.

Notice that Allison is thinking about her audience in each case, rather than the subject of her presentation. Each objective involved changing her audience in some way.

Ted and Adam are good at defining their objectives, but they have difficulty achieving them because they do not have an effective method of selecting content.

Ted: Once I know what I want my presentation to achieve, I make detailed notes on the subject.

Giving Successful Presentations

Adam: Me, too. It takes a long time, but it's worth it.

Ted: I agree. You won't achieve your objective unless you cover the subject in detail.

Only when you are clear about why you are making your presentation, should you turn your attention to selecting and organizing the content. The content of your presentation is what you will say in order to achieve your objective.

Ted and Adam write detailed notes which cover as much of the subject matter as possible. As they say, this is time consuming. Yet it doesn't actually guarantee that they select the correct content for their audiences. Ted and Adam are keen to learn a more efficient way of preparing. They watch Allison, and are impressed by how well her presentation content suits her objective. They ask her how she selects it.

Choose quickly

"I don't labor over my content; I choose it very quickly. This helps my ideas to flow, and also saves me time."

Create outline

"I identify my main points first, and then connected sub-points. I write them as notes--single words and phrases--not sentences."

As Allison shows, the best way to select content is to work quickly, giving yourself an overview in the form of very brief main points and sub-points.

The last stage of the preparation process is organizing your content for your audience. The content needs to be put in a logical order, with the main points grouped together, supported by the sub-points.

Arrange in logical order

Ask yourself: "What order of content will be best for my audience?" For example, one logical way of organizing content is chronological, presenting content about the past first, before moving to the present, and finally the future.

Group your main points

Group your main points in a way that follows your logical order. So, for example, if you have three main points to make about a past issue, deal with them one after the other, in the order in which they happened.

Choose powerful sub-points

Your sub-points are secondary content. Do not try to include all of them at the organization stage. Include only limited content--for example, facts or illustrative case studies--to support each main point. Do not overload your audience with secondary content.

Question

Milenka is desperate. She is so busy, and now she must prepare a presentation that she wasn't expecting. She knows that there are three preparation stages, but not what is involved in each. Help Milenka by matching each stage to one or more appropriate descriptions.

Options:

A. Identify the objective.
B. Select the content.
C. Organize the content.

Targets:

1. Identify the main points and sub-points.
2. Decide how you want the audience to be changed as a result of the presentation.
3. Group your main points, supported by strong but brief secondary content.
4. Put your material in a logical order.

5. Write brief notes, in the form of an overview of the main points and sub-points.
Answer:
First, base your objective on how you want your audience to change. Then select main points and sub-points quickly and make brief notes. Finally, group your main points and brief sub-points in a logical order.

An efficient way of selecting the content is to identify the main point and sub-points quickly. Milenka can quickly list these out by using single words or phrases, not sentences. This will make her more efficient and give her presentation better flow.

When Milenka decides what she wants the end result to be, she will have identified the objective of the presentation. This will keep her focused when it comes to selecting and organizing the content.

Once the content has been selected, Milenka can organize it by deciding what the main points and supporting pieces are. The secondary supporting pieces should be strong so as to avoid overload.

Deciding on a logical order for the content is an important part of organizing it. Milenka will need to ask herself what sort of order makes sense for her audience.

By writing a very quick overview using brief notes, Milenka can efficiently select the content she will use. This process generates a natural flow and selection of material that will make her presentation seem smooth.

Ted and Adam were impressed with Allison's advice about how to select their content. But when they went away and put it into practice independently, they found that they used two different approaches, both of which seemed to work.

Brainstorm

Ted noted main points and sub-points randomly on a page, as they occurred to him. He didn't try to complete all sub-points before moving on to another main point, but jumped back and forth. He generated a lot of content very quickly.

Linear list

Adam wrote the first main point that he thought of at the top of a piece of paper, and listed all of the sub-points under it, very fast, as a set of bullet points. Then he wrote the next main point, and its sub-points, and so on.

Both brainstorming and making a linear list work as ways of selecting content. However, brainstorming is preferable because it encourages a more flexible and imaginative approach to finding content.

Adam now wants to discuss how he is going to organize his presentation, so he calls in on Ted, who is happy to act as a sounding board.

Adam: Looking at my content, I figure that the most logical organization for this presentation is a three-part structure.

Ted: What are the three parts?

Adam: I need to start by talking about our range of technologies. The next main part is a close look at some projects where our technologies have met the needs of specific clients. The final part is "What Integrated Solutions Can Offer You."

Ted: That sounds good. So, can you see the main headings that you can group together in the first part of the presentation?

Adam: Yes, I think that's easy. We have three current technologies serving different markets, and I'll focus on each one in turn.

Ted: Great! But looking at your notes, you seem to have a lot of secondary material on each technology.

Adam: I'm not going to cover everything--that's why we have brochures! I'm only going to talk in detail about the main feature of each technology.

Adam has grasped how to organize his content well. His points follow a logical order, moving from general features, to examples, to content specific to the audience-- in this case, the client.

He then groups main points together under these three sections, supporting them with strong examples. But he doesn't just throw in all of his supporting data, because this would overload the audience. He chooses it carefully.

Case Study: Question 1 of 3
Scenario

For your convenience, the case study is repeated with each question.

In tandem with Mai, you have introduced a new customer support process to Cook Autoservices to improve customer satisfaction levels. But the new process isn't being followed properly. You and Mai need to make a presentation to get the customer support department back on track.

Show how you will prepare your presentation content by answering the following questions, in order.

Question

You work in a different office from Mai, so you send her an e-mail about how the two of you should begin preparing your presentation. What should your e-mail best say?

Options:

1. "I want to begin by describing the three elements of the customer support process on a set of slides."

2. "I've just finished a report on the strategic benefits of the new customer support process. We should start by reading that."

3. "The first thing to do is to focus on the details of the customer support process, so that we can explain them clearly."

4. "The first thing that we need to do is decide how we want this presentation to change behavior in the department. Everyone needs to follow the process to improve customer satisfaction."

Answer:

First, you need to be clear about your objective: in other words, how you want the customer support department to change as a result of your presentation.

Option 1: This choice is incorrect. The first step is to identify the objective of the presentation. You should make sure you and Mai are on the same page. After that, you can then focus on the steps of selecting and organizing content.

Option 2: This is an incorrect choice. You should first talk with Mai about identifying the objective. The two of you should state what results you want to see. Then you can decide how you want to handle secondary content.

Option 3: This choice is incorrect. The first thing to do is define the objective. Once you and Mai have articulated that, you can then begin selecting and organizing the content for maximum effectiveness.

Option 4: This is the correct choice. The first step is to identify the objective, which means stating what results you want to see. After you and Mai have identified the objective, you can then move to the content of the presentation.

Case Study: Question 2 of 3

Now you drive to Mai's office so that you can do some more work on the presentation. You want to select the presentation content now. What do you suggest to Mai?

Options:

1. "The presentation should start with information about face-to-face support. I'll write down what we'll say."

2. "Let's throw some random ideas up on your whiteboard here. We can use a pen each."

3. "I'll start by writing 'face-to-face support' here, and then we can quickly add anything that falls under that heading before moving on."

4. "I've kept the whole day free, so that we can cover the entire subject."

5. "I'll dictate stuff about telephone support, then you can do the same for routine maintenance, and then we can transcribe it."

Answer:

The second step is to quickly select content, either by brainstorming or by producing a linear list. You're not ordering the content yet, dictating wastes time, and you don't need to cover the whole subject, only the relevant information.

Option 1: This is an incorrect choice. This statement focuses on organizing the content. Before you can determine what is covered first, you and Mai should select the main and sub-points of the content.

Option 2: This is a correct choice. This statement suggests the brainstorming approach, which can quickly generate content. This will help you and Mai select the most salient content to cover.

Option 3: This choice is correct. This statement suggest a linear list approach to selecting the content. This helps the content fall into place quickly without determining the organization too early.

Option 4: This is an incorrect choice. The process of selecting the content should flow fairly quickly. This statement would take too much time and generate an amount of content that is unrealistic to cover.

Option 5: This choice is incorrect. This approach would generate too much detail and would be highly inefficient. You should suggest to Mai that you both select the content by either brainstorming or developing a quick linear list.

Case Study: Question 3 of 3

You have identified your presentation content, and now it is time for the last step. What do you say to Mai now?

Options:

1. "The breakdown in communication when Jed failed to log his site visit is a perfect example. Let's use that."

2. "We have heaps of examples of failures to respond correctly. Let's list them all one after the other so people really get it."

3. "We have a heading 'Lost Business,' so let's add in brief supporting data here."

4. "We can follow the same format as my marketing report."

Giving Successful Presentations

5. "Let's start with a slide headed 'Failures of the Old System' and then move on to how the process will improve each step."
Answer:
You need to arrange your content in a way that helps your audience to understand it in a presentation situation. Support your main points with brief secondary data, but don't overload your audience with too much repetition.

Option 1: This is a correct choice. When organizing the content, you and Mai should choose the examples that support the main points best. This example illustrates the point, but will keep your presentation concise.

Option 2: This is an incorrect choice. You do not want to overwhelm your audience. Instead, you and Mai should choose the facts and stories that best illustrate your points. Keep your secondary information strong but concise.

Option 3: This is a correct choice. Once you've brainstormed the content, you and Mai can add in the supporting data. This process and the points should be kept brief and most pertinent.

Option 4: This is an incorrect choice. The marketing report had a different purpose, so its organization may not make sense here. The organization for the presentation by you and Mai should fit the objective and selected content already identified.

Option 5: This is a correct choice. After the content has been selected, you and Mai are ready to begin organizing the presentation. This statement suggests a chronological approach for organization, which is logical.

The purpose of your presentation is not simply to go through all of the data relating to the new customer support procedures. It's to focus on the parts of the process that your colleagues are not following. Producing brief notes about content to begin with will encourage you to put only the relevant ideas on paper.

Using good case studies is an excellent way to highlight the behavior that needs to change, but you don't need a whole lot of similar examples to make your point.

Don't try to say everything in your presentation. Help your audience out by selecting bite-sized pieces of relevant content, arranged in a logical order that will make the most sense to people.

METHODS TO ORGANIZE PRESENTATION NOTES

Methods to organize presentation notes

You know what you want to say in your presentation, but how can you make sure you remember it when faced with your audience? It's all in how you organize your notes.

Organize them in the right way, and it boosts your confidence. Choose the wrong method, and all of your hard preparation work will have been wasted. Karl decided to learn his presentation by heart. This is not a good idea, because you are likely to forget something important.

Instead of trying to remember your presentation, make notes. There are three main methods for organizing your written notes, all of which you will use with varying frequency. They are:
- usually--main headings with sub-point bullets,
- sometimes--main headings alone,
- occasionally--a full speech.

Your presentation notes do two things. They provide you with prompts, so that you deliver your message properly. They also allow you to sound natural when talking to your audience.

Question

Rina is considering the main methods for organizing notes, and wants to know what the most and least common methods are. Help Rina by matching the appropriate frequency of use to each approach.

Options:

A. usually
B. sometimes
C. occasionally

Targets:

1. Read the presentation as a speech.
2. Use main headings and bulleted lists of sub-points.
3. Use main headings alone.

Answer:

Most of the time your notes will be in the form of main points and bulleted sub-points, with less frequent use of main headings alone and full speeches. Never learn your presentations by heart.

If every word needs to be exact, Rina might be in one of the rare situations in which she needs to write out the entire speech and read it directly from notes. However, this will occur only occasionally.

Most of the time, Rina will only need main headings and bulleted lists of sub-points. These will jog her memory but keep her from getting mired in too much detail or sounding too flat. This is what Rina will usually need to do.

When Rina knows she won't forget something important or has given the same presentation many times, she can rely on main headings alone. This will happen sometimes, but not often.

Speakers often select their approach to notes for the wrong reason. They feel anxious, so they try to give themselves security by writing their presentation out as a full speech, or making notes so detailed that they are almost like a speech. Don't take this tempting road--use headings and bullet points to clarify your thinking, unless you really need a detailed speech.

Lily is an experienced presenter who knows that the right notes help her to deliver the goods to her audiences. She uses each of the three legitimate approaches to notes, and never tries to do without notes altogether.

Main headings and bullets

This is the best approach for when Lily has an important or complicated presentation, or is not familiar with the content. It ensures that she covers everything, and that her voice sounds natural, since she isn't reading a speech straight out.

Read a speech

Lily knows that when she delivers a speech, it can sound flat, no matter how hard she tries. But occasionally, if legal liability is an issue, then every word has to be exact. Then she might have no choice but to read a speech.

Main headings only

If it's a presentation that Lily has given many times before, or the content is not too complicated, then she's happy with just a list of main headings. She only uses this when she knows that she won't forget anything important.

Lily's approach overall is to use the minimum amount of notes possible. The more notes she has, the more time she has to spend reading them. Follow Lily's example, and use only the details that you absolutely need.

Question

Your colleague, Vera, believes that how you organize presentation notes depends on the presentation context. She makes a list of note organization methods and the contexts that suit each. Unfortunately, her list has been deleted. Rewrite it by matching each method with its appropriate context.

Options:

A. main headings and sub-point bullets
B. a speech
C. main headings only

Targets:

1. a precise presentation with important legal consequences
2. a relatively simple or familiar presentation
3. a significant presentation, or when you don't know the content well

Answer:

Actually, if it's an important presentation, you need main headings and sub-points. For a simple presentation, you can use more limited notes. If there are legal implications, you should read a full speech.

When every word counts, as in legal matters, it is important to write out the entire speech and deliver it from notes. This way Vera won't leave out anything important and will get the wording correct.

If Vera has done this presentation many times before, or if the content is fairly simple, Vera can jot down main headings only. The main headings can jog her memory, but it's not necessary to include much detail.

Usually, Vera will be giving a new presentation or be somewhat unfamiliar with the content. In these instances, she will need to list out main headings and sub-points as bullets. This ensures she covers everything but doesn't sound flat.

You need to decide which of the three note organization methods to choose on a case-by-case basis. See if you can choose correctly in the following scenario.

How well did you manage your note organization methods? Some of Aaron's comments were helpful, and some were off the mark. For very important presentations, or new and unfamiliar content, main headings and sub-points will ensure that you don't forget anything important.

For simple or familiar content, you can usually get away with main headings only. But if your words have legal implications, or will be reported by the media, then you need to get them right. A prepared speech is the way to go.

If you are making a prepared policy statement to government on behalf of the association, it's best to read from it directly, so that nothing is misunderstood. However, when talking about your complex research, you will need to rely on quite detailed slides. The other two presentations are more straightforward--you know the subject matter well, and neither will take long. Main headings will be enough for these.

Most speakers use more notes than they really require. Match your note-making approach to the expected precision of your content, and your familiarity with it. Your talks will be accurate, but still flow naturally.

SECTION 3 - CONTROLLING YOURSELF AND YOUR ENVIRONMENT

SECTION 3 - Controlling Yourself and Your Environment

When it comes to presenting, leave little to chance. Your state of mind and your immediate environment affect how successful a presentation will be. Aim to control them as much as possible. Some nerves are natural before an important presentation. They may even help your thought process, but only if you master them. Likewise, you can't control every aspect of your speaking environment, but you can seek to exert a positive influence over it.

Do you get "butterflies," or nerves, in your stomach before presentations? If not, you're lucky. If you do, you're in the majority. Most speakers experience some anxiety before a presentation. If you ask people why, they will give you a variety of reasons--some rational, some not.

Feeling a little tense before a presentation isn't a problem. On the contrary, it can contribute a positive energy to your presentation. Presentation anxiety is most common on the morning of the presentation, and in the few minutes immediately before you speak, so it is at these times that you need to control your nerves the most.

When you have prepared your presentation, you need to rehearse it, so that when you stand up in front of your audience you deliver it exactly as you planned to. The success of your presentation doesn't just depend on good preparation and rehearsal. You need to control the presentation environment as much as possible.

Your presentation environment is the room that you are speaking in. Exert as much control as you can over

- the arrangement of seating,
- the position of equipment,
- the shape and size of the room.

CONTROLING ANXIETY AND THE PRESENTATION ENVIRONMENT

Controlling anxiety and the presentation environment

When it comes to presenting, leave little to chance. Your state of mind and your immediate environment affect how successful a presentation will be. Aim to control them as much as possible.

Some nerves are natural before an important presentation. They may even help your thought process, but only if you master them. Likewise, you can't control every aspect of your speaking environment, but you can seek to exert a positive influence over it.

Calvin did nothing to take charge of his own state of mind, or of his environment. As he explains to Abby, his presentation went very badly.

Calvin: I was so anxious, even before I got there, that I had no confidence. Abby: Haven't you learned any techniques for controlling your nerves? Calvin: No.

Abby: You should. It would help.

Calvin: Well, even if I wasn't nervous at first, the room would still have unsettled me. It was too small, and it didn't have the equipment that I wanted. I just couldn't communicate my message properly.

Calvin was a victim of his own anxiety, and the fact that he was ill-informed about his venue. Controlling himself and his environment would not necessarily have guaranteed that his audience enjoyed his presentation, but at least he would have had a better chance of holding their attention. People pick up on a speaker's nerves, which can be distracting. Missing or faulty equipment, space restrictions, and temperature, lighting, or seating issues will all take your listeners' minds off what you are saying.

In this lesson, you will learn how to take control of these factors. Not only will this help you to keep your audience's attention, but you can reduce your own anxiety, which will help you to remain focused on your audience, and therefore to communicate your message properly.

Question

Your colleagues are not convinced that there's any reason to consider their state of mind or environment when giving presentations. You disagree, because you know the benefits of exerting control over these factors. What do you say to change your colleagues' minds?

Options:

1. "You can focus on your audience better."
2. "The audience will be able to focus on your message."
3. "Your audience will enjoy your presentation."
4. "You will be better able to communicate your message."

Giving Successful Presentations

5. "You can reduce your anxiety levels."
6. "The audience will approve of your equipment."
Answer:
In fact, the correct answers are shown. Controlling your inner and outer environments will ensure that both you and your audience remain focused on the task at hand--transmitting and receiving your message.

Option 1: This is a correct choice. By controlling their nerves, your colleagues will be better able to focus on the audience. This will allow them to deliver their messages better, which should result in better attention from the audience.

Option 2: Correct. People in the audience pick up on a presenter's nerves or other distractions, such as faulty equipment or a poor environment. By controlling themselves and the environment, your colleagues will have better presentations.

Option 3: This is an incorrect choice. Controlling yourself and your environment does not necessarily mean the audience will enjoy the presentation. It does mean, however, that your colleagues can have better audience attention.

Option 4: This choice is correct. When your colleagues can reduce their anxiety, they will focus better on the audience and message. This will help them communicate their message better.

Option 5: This is a correct choice. Taking control of matters and maintaining focus can help your colleagues reduce their level of anxiety. This in turn helps them give a better presentation and gain better audience attention.

Option 6: This is an incorrect choice. The audience may disapprove of your equipment regardless. But by exerting control over themselves and the environment, your colleagues will help their audiences pay more attention to their messages.

In this lesson, you will discover some of the techniques and tips that allow you to control your anxiety and positively influence your speaking environment. They won't make your message better, but they will improve its reception.

IRRATIONAL PRESENTATION AND RATIONAL RESPONSES

Irrational presentation and rational responses

Do you get "butterflies," or nerves, in your stomach before presentations? If not, you're lucky. If you do, you're in the majority. Most speakers experience some anxiety before a presentation.

If you ask people why, they will give you a variety of reasons--some rational, some not. Esther and Hannah were certainly not calm before their presentations, but their reasons are rational.

Esther: My presentation this morning went well, but those butterflies were jumping around in my stomach.

Hannah: Well, you've only done a few presentations. I've given a lot, but still get a little anxious if there's a lot riding on my talk.

Esther: Like your presentation to the Board last week?

Hannah: Yeah! They said that I did a good job, but there were a few nerves--though nothing I didn't know how to control.

Esther: I feel anxious because I'm on my own up there when I'm speaking. There's just me and everybody looking at me and expecting me to come up with the goods.

Hannah: I know. A presentation is a great opportunity to make your mark, but as a presenter there's a lot of pressure on you.

It's not surprising that Esther and Hannah were anxious. If you're an inexperienced presenter, or it's a very important presentation, then you're bound to get nervous. Or perhaps you can handle a small group of people, but balk at speaking to a large audience in a big auditorium. In these situations, nerves are par for the book. But you can control them.

Question

Your colleagues list various reasons why a speaker may feel anxious before a presentation. What are the rational reasons?

Options:

1. It is a very important presentation.
2. The speaker is inexperienced.
3. The subject is ground-breaking.
4. The audience and venue are large.
5. It is a new audience.

Answer:

Nerves are par for the book when there is a lot riding on your talk, when you're an inexperienced presenter, or when the venue and audience are large.

Option 1: This is a correct choice. Even an experienced presenter can still get nervous if there's a lot riding on a presentation. Feeling anxious about high-profile presentations is rational.

Giving Successful Presentations

Option 2: This is a correct choice. A person who has had only a few or no opportunities to present will be naturally more nervous than a person who has given many presentations. With more experience, a person can expect to become less nervous.

Option 3: This is an incorrect choice. The subject of a presentation should not be anxiety inducing. Rational reasons for feeling anxious include lack of experience, the size of the audience, or the import of the presentation.

Option 4: This is a correct choice. Many people may be comfortable speaking to a small group but become nervous in front of a larger audience. This is a rational source of anxiety that can be controlled.

Option 5: This is an incorrect choice. In a sense, every audience is a new one. However, most people have rational fears over the size of the audience, not its makeup. Generally, audiences want to see you do well.

Some presentation anxieties are rational. But others make little or no sense. Irrational anxieties are those things that people concern themselves about that are highly unlikely to happen.

There are several irrational pre-presentation anxieties. Joseph has a presentation coming up, and three things are bothering him. As his colleague, Angela, shows him, they are all irrational concerns.

They won't like me

"I get nervous in case the audience just doesn't like me, and people start to react in a hostile way."

Response 1

"Why wouldn't people like you? They want you to succeed, and they are prepared to like you, even if your message is one that they don't want to hear."

I'll run out of material

"I worry that I won't have enough to say. I'm supposed to talk for twenty minutes, and I'm afraid that I'll run out of material after fifteen minutes."

Response 2

"Subject experts like you never run out of material. Provided that you know your subject well, you will have more than enough to say to occupy twenty minutes."

I'll forget

"I have this fear that I will be standing there, in the middle of my presentation, and suddenly I will completely forget what to say."

Response 3

"Provided that you prepare your presentation properly, you won't forget. You will have notes, remember, and slides. They will always prompt you."

Angela is right. There is no reason to worry that your audience will feel negative about you, or that you will run out of material, or that you will forget what you want to say. On the contrary:
- your audience wants you to succeed,
- you'll have too much to say, rather than too little,
- with notes, you can't forget anything.

Question

Wyatt is frantic. He is preparing his sales presentation for tomorrow, but can't stop fretting about what might go wrong. You can see that his anxieties are irrational, and so you try to reassure him. Match each of Wyatt's concerns with your most appropriate good advice.

Options:

A. "The audience won't like me!"
B. "I will run out of things to say!"

C. "I will forget everything!"

Targets:

1. "The audience wants you to succeed."
2. "You have made good notes."
3. "If you know your subject, that won't happen."

Answer:

It's important not to let irrational fears run away with you. If you are well prepared, then these concerns can't manifest.

The audience is usually prepared to like you the presenter, even if they don't like your topic. Understanding that the audience wants him to succeed will address Wyatt's fear about not being liked by the audience.

If Wyatt has good notes with him he won't be able to forget everything. Wyatt will probably have to consult his notes, but that doesn't mean he forgot. The notes will keep him on track.

When you know what you're talking about, you usually have more things to say than you can possibly fit into the presentation. Since Wyatt knows his subject, he'll have more to say than he can, not less.

Distinguishing between rational and irrational presentation anxieties is the first step towards controlling them. If you know what you face, you can use the right techniques to conquer your fears successfully.

ANXIETY-CONTROL TECHNIQUES

Anxiety-control techniques

Feeling a little tense before a presentation isn't a problem. On the contrary, it can contribute a positive energy to your presentation. Presentation anxiety is most common on the morning of the presentation, and in the few minutes immediately before you speak, so it is at these times that you need to control your nerves the most.

Doreen knows exactly what the results of anxiety are, as she tells Gabby.

Doreen: Every time I sit on the stage with a major presentation to make, I feel the same way.

Gabby: How?

Doreen: Well, my heart rate increases, my breathing is rapid and shallow, and I can't seem to control my thoughts.

Gabby: I've often seen you speak, and those signs are not obvious to me.

Doreen: I know. I'm aware of these things, but I overcome the feelings, and the audience is none the wiser.

Question

How does presentation anxiety manifest?
Options:
1. The presenter suffers from rapid and shallow breathing.
2. The presenter feels an increased heart rate.
3. The audience responds negatively.
4. The presenter cannot control his or her thoughts.
5. The presenter will never deliver the presentation effectively.

Answer:
Anxiety affects the presenter's breathing, heart rate, and ability to think clearly. These effects are not obvious to an audience, nor do they affect delivery if the presenter can control them.

Option 1: This is a correct choice. Physical manifestations of anxiety may include rapid and shallow breathing. However, if you are aware of these, you can control them.

Option 2: This choice is correct. When you are anxious, your heart rate will increase enough that you may feel it. However, by focusing and relaxing, you can keep this under control, and the audience won't know the difference.

Option 3: This is an incorrect choice. Signs of anxiety are internal factors a person can control, not external factors such as audience response. Anxiety is manifest through rapid or shallow breathing, increased heart rate, and lack of focus.

Option 4: This is a correct choice. When you feel like you cannot control your thoughts, you are probably experiencing some anxiety just prior to your presentation.

However, by regaining focus and relaxing, you can regain control.

Option 5: This is an incorrect choice. Many speakers often have signs of anxiety, like rapid and shallow breathing, increased heart rate, and lack of control over thoughts. However, many still deliver their presentations and keep these under control.

If not dealt with properly, presentation anxiety can affect the delivery of your message. You need a strategy to control it.

A two-part strategy can help you to take charge of your mind and body when you give presentations. The strategy involves:
- minimizing anxiety in the preceding hours,
- calming yourself just before your presentation.

Raymond has a conference speech to deliver this morning. He thinks about how to control his anxiety. First, he needs to reduce anxiety in the hours leading up to the presentation, and then strive to remain calm immediately before speaking.

The hours before

"Most of the morning I will spend on normal work, but I will make sure that I get some exercise, and also find time to relax."

Immediately before

"Just before I speak, I will sit or stand comfortably, try to control my breathing, and get rid of irrational thoughts."

Question

You are impressed with Sonya. She gives a lot of important sales presentations, and although she is often pitching to people more senior than herself, she never

Giving Successful Presentations

seems worried. You ask her how she controls her anxiety. Match the two time periods to one or more of Sonya's comments.

Options:
A. the hours before the presentation
B. immediately before the presentation

Targets:
1. "I make a point of finding time to relax."
2. "I get some exercise."
3. "I adopt a comfortable posture, and get rid of anxious thoughts."
4. "I work normally."
5. "I control my breathing."

Answer:
Actually, in the morning you should do normal work, go for a walk, or take time to sit quietly. Just before the presentation, breathe deeply and relax your body. Also, make sure that you are sitting or standing comfortably.

It is easiest to find time to relax in the hours before the presentation. At some point during those hours, Sonya finds a way to relax.

Exercise is easiest to fit in during a few hours before the presentation instead of trying to do it immediately before. Sonya will use the time frame of a few hours to get in some exercise.

Anxious thoughts will normally creep in just before the presentation. Sonya handles this immediately before the presentation by adopting a comfortable posture and silencing anxious thoughts.

Since work takes time, and she has some time to give, Sonya will work normally in the hours before the presentation. She will conduct her more routine tasks instead of allowing herself to build anxiety.

Controlled breathing may not last several hours, so Sonya will control her breathing just immediately before the presentation. That way, she can enter the presentation with smooth and steady breathing.

A lot of people spend the hours before they speak rehearsing their presentation, or doing other stressful or demanding work. This only generates anxiety. It is much better to follow Sonya's example, and keep to routine tasks.

Bill has a major client presentation to give this afternoon, but because he follows the correct strategy, he has no difficulty keeping his anxiety in check throughout the morning.

Routine tasks

"I'll spend some time calling the rest of the team to schedule some meetings. I have also got site visit reports to write up, so I'll do that. I'll postpone the disciplinary reviews though, since I don't want to do any stressful work today."

Exercise

"I'll walk to the store to pick up a sandwich, instead of driving. It's a nice day."

Relax

"I think that I'll go to the meeting room at the end of the corridor, so no one will disturb me. I can just sit and unwind for a few moments. And when I get to the venue, I'll relax in my car for a minute before going in."

Once Bill gets to his presentation room, he still manages to remain calm just before he speaks.

Sit comfortably

"When I'm sitting, I make sure that my back is straight and supported, and my body is not twisted in my chair. I rest my hands in my lap, and put my feet on the ground. I don't cross my legs. If standing, I do so with my feet a little way apart. I don't put one foot in front of the other."

Control your breathing

"I take a deep breath for a slow count of five, hold it, and then breathe out for a count of five. Basically, I fill my lungs with air, before emptying them slowly."

Get rid of anxious thoughts

"I don't think of anything that can produce anxiety. I imagine that I'm in a place that is very relaxing, like my favorite armchair at home."

The strategy you have learned for controlling anxiety is a simple one. You will develop confidence in it by using it as much as possible. You may not completely eliminate all anxiety before a really important presentation. But you can minimize it, which will allow you to benefit from the positive aspects of tension, and not suffer from its negative effects.

REHEARSAL TECHNIQUES

Rehearsal techniques

When you have prepared your presentation, you need to rehearse it, so that when you stand up in front of your audience you deliver it exactly as you planned to.

But how do you rehearse? How much time do you spend? Don't rehearse like Justin, who is driving to work. His idea of presentation rehearsal is completely unrealistic.

Doreen: Now, I'll just read these notes quickly while I'm at the traffic lights. I've got about ten minutes until I get to work.

Doreen: Nice song! I like this song.

Doreen: The lights are green, buddy! Get moving!

The more realistic your presentation rehearsal is, the more successful it will be. To ensure that your presentation rehearsal is effective:
- rehearse straight after preparing your presentation,
- rehearse several times,
- simulate the real presentation conditions.

Giving Successful Presentations

Question

You are planning to spend more time rehearsing your presentations, as you think that it will improve them. But you want to ensure that your rehearsal time is effective. What should you do?

Options:

1. Rehearse a few moments before you present, in the actual venue.
2. Rehearse after you have finished preparing your presentation.
3. Rehearse your presentation once.
4. Rehearse your presentation several times.
5. Make your rehearsal as realistic as possible.

Answer:

Actually, the correct answers are shown. It is important to make your rehearsals simulate reality as closely as possible, but don't leave it until the last minute just to do it in the actual venue.

Option 1: This is an incorrect choice. You should rehearse right after preparing the presentation. You should also rehearse it several times. Waiting until just before may not give you any time at all.

Option 2: This choice is correct. You should rehearse right after you finish preparing your presentation. This will reinforce the content and allow you time for multiple rehearsals.

Option 3: This choice is incorrect. You should rehearse your presentation more than once. This will give you more practice and make you feel more comfortable.

Option 4: This is a correct choice. Rehearsing multiple times is definitely a good way to practice. This will help you feel more relaxed with the content and delivery.

Option 5: This choice is correct. To make your rehearsal realistic, you should simulate the actual presenting conditions. This will help you deliver your presentation exactly as you planned to.

Effective presentation rehearsals can take one of two forms: a full rehearsal, or a partial rehearsal. Edna and Luther are experienced presenters. They are comparing notes about how they make their full presentation rehearsals effective.

Edna: If it's a twenty-minute speech, I try to rehearse it in twenty minutes. Two or three full rehearsals allow me to get the timing right.

Luther: Another important thing is to rehearse in a space that is similar in size to the actual presentation venue.

Edna: And also to rehearse with your slides and any other equipment that you'll be using.

Luther: Yeah, that's really important.

In order for a full rehearsal to be realistic, you should:
- deliver it in the correct amount of time,
- include your slides and other equipment,
- use a space that is a similar size to your venue.

Edna and Luther know that, in addition to rehearsing their presentations in full, they should also do some partial rehearsals.

Difficult parts

"Some parts of the presentation are more difficult than others. I like to verbally rehearse the most demanding parts more often."

Movements

"Movements and gestures are more important in some parts of the presentation--I practice these over and over to get them right."

Question

Greg has spent a lot of time rehearsing Friday's presentation, both fully and partially. Match Greg's two approaches to rehearsing to one or more of his comments.

Options:

A. full rehearsal

B. partial rehearsal

Targets:

1. "I rehearsed in a room which is similar to the presentation room."

2. "I delivered the presentation in the correct period of time."

3. "I rehearsed the actions for the parts of the presentation that I find difficult."

4. "I went through the presentation using all of my slides and other equipment."

5. "I rehearsed the words for the sections of the presentation that I find difficult."

Answer:

In fact, a full rehearsal involves practicing the whole presentation in a room that is similar to the venue, with real visual aids, and ideally with an audience. A partial rehearsal involves focusing on difficult sections of the presentation.

By matching the size of the room for rehearsal to where he'll actually be presenting, Greg is doing a full rehearsal. This gives him a feel for the space and how to use it during his presentation.

By rehearsing the full presentation for the same amount of time as the actual presentation, Greg is doing a full rehearsal. This gives him a feel for how he wants to use the time and how the presentation is fitting into the time.

By focusing on only key parts, Greg is doing a partial rehearsal. Instead of working on the entire thing, he's smoothing out the rougher parts.

A good approach for a full rehearsal is to use any equipment you'll actually be using during the presentation. By doing this, Greg gets a feel for how to work the equipment and how the entire presentation will go.

When Greg focuses in on key sections, he is doing a partial rehearsal. Partial rehearsals are good for zoning in on the harder parts and smoothing them out.

Ralph has been making presentations for years, as a key account manager with Pinnacle Computer Systems. His last presentation was to the finance department of his biggest client, TSC Broadcasting, so he had to ensure that it went well. He undertook several full rehearsals in the days leading up to his presentation.

Room-size assessment

"I rehearsed in our biggest meeting room, which is similar in size to the room at TSC. I pushed the table back so that I had more space to move around, the way that I knew it would be at TSC's."

Equipment positioning

"I rehearsed with my computer, the screen, and a flipchart in the same positions and the same distance apart that they were going to be at TSC."

Colleague feedback

"I rehearsed the whole presentation three times. I asked my colleague, Jane, to sit through it and time it for me. She also gave me feedback. The first time, the talk was too long, so I removed a couple of examples."

In order to judge how effective your presentation is in your chosen rehearsal space, it is also good to rehearse in front of an audience. You could either ask some colleagues to provide feedback, or record your presentation on a video camera and then play it back.

As well as doing several full rehearsals of his TSC presentation, Ralph took every opportunity that he could find in the days leading up to it to do some partial rehearsals of the difficult sections.

Rehearsing the words

"I sat at my desk and rehearsed in my head the exact words that I was going to use at the start and end of the presentation. I also mentally rehearsed my introductions of each key point, because those are difficult moments, and they have to be right."

Rehearsing the movements

"I spent time in front of a mirror, practicing gestures and facial expressions that emphasize the most vital points. I also rehearsed how I would point at the screen during certain sections, and even how to get the slides in and out, to ensure that I did not disrupt my timing or delivery."

Which of these rehearsal techniques have you tried? What could you do to improve the quality of your presentation rehearsals? Test yourself in the following scenario.

Case Study: Question 1 of 3
Scenario

For your convenience, the case study is repeated with each question.

You are head of finance for Parkers Stores. Today is Monday. On Friday, you are presenting the financial results for the last six months to the store managers in the large meeting room at corporate headquarters, which is on the other side of town. You have spent a lot of time preparing your presentation. You plan to talk for thirty minutes, with slides, and then show a short video from the chief executive, before finishing off with a brainstorming session.

Show how you will rehearse your presentation by answering the following questions in order.

Question

You've set Tuesday afternoon aside for full rehearsals of your presentation. You decide to rehearse in the staff cafeteria, since it's the largest room available. Which of the following things do you do?

Options:

1. Set up the projector so the slides project on the only blank wall in the cafeteria.

2. Rehearse using the slides and working the video, with everything set up as it will be on the day.

3. Remove all of the tables and chairs from the cafeteria, to make more space.

4. Move the chairs into a configuration that is similar to that at the venue.

5. Decide to check the video on the presentation day, since the chief executive's message isn't ready yet.

Answer:

In fact, you want to position and use all of your equipment in exactly the same way as you will position and use it on the day. And you want the room to be set up in a similar way to the real venue. All venues will have chairs.

Option 1: This is an incorrect choice. You should rehearse using the slides, not just projecting them. You should also arrange the equipment exactly how you will use it, not adapt it to the practice space.

Option 2: This is a correct choice. As part of your full rehearsal, you should use all the equipment exactly as you will use it during the actual presentation. This will give you a good feel and help you identify any problems early.

Option 3: This is an incorrect choice. Moving chairs entirely does not simulate the space you'll be in. Instead, arrange the chairs as they'll appear in your actual venue.

Option 4: This is a correct choice. The size of the cafeteria simulates the size of the actual venue, so you can simulate the arrangement by moving chairs. This will give you a feel for the space.

Option 5: This is an incorrect choice. You should check any technology well before the presentation day in case adjustments should be made. By waiting until that day, you may lose out on making any corrections.

Case Study: Question 2 of 3

Your assistant Sheryl now interrupts you, and asks if there's anything that you need. What do you best say to her?

Options:

1. "Just a cup of coffee, thanks."

2. "Actually, could you help me to move those last two tables out? That would be great."

3. "Could you let me know when it's three o'clock? That would help with my timing."

4. "Actually, can you sit through one rehearsal, and time it for me?"

5. "Can you stay out there and make sure that no one disturbs me for the next half an hour?"

Answer:

You need to time your rehearsal properly, and it's a good idea to get someone to act as an audience, so that you can gain some feedback.

Option 1: This choice is incorrect. Having Sheryl watch your presentation would be very helpful. She can give you feedback that will help you refine your presentation.

Option 2: This choice is incorrect. A better use of Sheryl's offer would be for her to watch your presentation. She may be able to help you refine your approach and time it to see if you run long or short.

Option 3: This is an incorrect choice. While this may give you a rough feel for the timing, Sheryl can't provide you any actual feedback. If she stays to watch you, she can give you feedback and tips on your use of the time.

Option 4: This is the correct choice. By sitting through one rehearsal, Sheryl can both give you feedback and time it for you. That way, you know how you can refine your presentation.

Option 5: This choice is incorrect. Sheryl could better spend her time watching you. That way, she can give you good feedback and time your presentation. Her input may help you refine and make your presentation all the better.

Case Study: Question 3 of 3

Before the big day, you also decide to partially rehearse your presentation on several occasions. Which of the following do you do?

Giving Successful Presentations

Options:

1. While sitting at your desk, mentally go over the verbal introduction to the chief executive's video.
2. Mentally practice the start and end of the presentation.
3. Rehearse by mentally repeating the whole presentation very quickly.
4. In front of your home mirror, work out the facial gestures that you'll use to open the brainstorming session.
5. At your office desk, think about your facial gestures and how you'll move around the stage.

Answer:

In fact, you should partially rehearse your presentation by repeating the words and actions that are particularly difficult or important. It's better to rehearse gestures in front of a mirror.

Option 1: This is a correct choice. The introduction of the video is a very important part, so it's worth going over this part to get it right. Any key part is worth rehearsing in isolation because the wording can be so important.

Option 2: This is a correct choice. The important parts of the presentation are worth practicing on their own. These are key points where you need to get your wording right.

Option 3: This is an incorrect choice. Partial rehearsal is targeted at really difficult or key pieces where wording is important. Instead of repeating the entire presentation, you should work on the key parts.

Option 4: This choice is correct. When you practice in front of a mirror, you can adjust any gestures or expressions. This will help you make sure you emphasize the right parts appropriately.

Option 5: This is an incorrect choice. Gestures should be practiced in front of a mirror. That way, you are sure they look the way you want them to. This will help you emphasize the key points well.

Rearranging the furniture in the cafeteria, and installing the equipment that you are going to use, creates the most realistic space in which to rehearse. Having an audience, and practicing your timing also adds to this sense of reality.

Practicing short but difficult sections of your presentation, both verbally and physically, is a powerful technique that will give your rehearsals a significant boost.

The more realistic your rehearsal is, the more effective it will be, improving your chances of successfully delivering your message, and boosting your confidence.

CONTROLLING THE PRESENTATION ENVIRONMENT

Controlling the presentation environment

The success of your presentation doesn't just depend on good preparation and rehearsal. You need to control the presentation environment as much as possible.

Your presentation environment is the room that you are speaking in. Exert as much control as you can over
- the arrangement of seating,
- the position of equipment,
- the shape and size of the room.

Question

You have a presentation coming up. You phone the presentation venue. What do you ask about in order to try to control your presentation environment?

Options:
1. the position of equipment
2. the arrangement of seats
3. the time the presentation begins
4. the size and shape of the room

5. the location of the venue

Answer:

Actually, you need to be concerned about the seating arrangement, position of equipment, and size and shape of the room.

Option 1: This is a correct choice. You can exert control over how the equipment is positioned. You want to achieve the best affect, so make sure everything is where you need and want it to be.

Option 2: This choice is correct. Seating arrangement can affect your presentation. Make sure seats are arranged in a way that best supports your presentation. You can exert control in this area.

Option 3: This is an incorrect choice. The time of the presentation is not an environmental factor. Although you should aim for an earlier time, this may not be in your control. You can arrange equipment and seats and request a good-sized room.

Option 4: This is a correct choice. You can request a particular size of room or one with a different shape if your venue does not suit your presentation. You should feel comfortable asking for what you need.

Option 5: This is an incorrect choice. You will need directions, but this is not an environmental factor. You can, however, control the position of equipment, arrangement of seats, and the size and shape of the room.

You can influence your presentation environment in two ways: by contacting the venue well in advance, and by arriving early on the day of your presentation to check that everything is acceptable. Naomi and Charles each gave a presentation yesterday. They are discussing how they tried to control their presentation environments.

Naomi: I contacted the conference organizers two weeks ago, and asked for dimensions of the auditorium and the stage. I also wanted to know what equipment there would be, and where I would be standing in relation to the screen.

Charles: Did everything go OK?

Naomi: Yes, in the end. But I sure am glad that I arrived an hour early, because the table and chairs were in the wrong position, and I had to get them moved, and some of the equipment that I had been promised was not there. The organizers had to get it and set it up.

Charles: My presentation was in this building, so I did not have to rely on someone else to set it up the way that I wanted. But I still arrived an hour before my presentation to make final adjustments to seating and equipment.

Naomi: I had a problem with my presentation last week. The room was way too small, and the shape obscured my demonstration. Luckily, I was able to change venues to a bigger hall.

Conrad always devotes time to checking the conditions in any room where he is presenting.

Seating arrangement

"I want the seats to be set out in a way that allows the audience to look at each other, and allows me to see everyone in the audience easily."

Position of equipment

"Any equipment has to be positioned so that it is convenient to use. If my words are most important, then I should be center stage, and not the equipment. If I'm demonstrating something vital using technology, then the equipment can be central."

Shape and size of room

"The room should be a comfortable size for the number of people in the audience, and of a shape that allows me to communicate with everyone."

There are some occasions when the seating arrangements or size of the venue are beyond your direct control.

But provided you discover this in advance, you can still exert indirect influence by modifying your presentation to accommodate the adverse conditions.

Question

You have made some notes for a talk called: "How to Control Your Presentation Environment." Match each room condition to one or more of your notes.

Options:

A. arrangement of seating
B. position of equipment
C. shape and size of room

Targets:

1. Most times, I must remain the center of attention.
2. Audience members have to be able to look at each other.
3. It has to be convenient to work with.
4. I need to be able to see each member of the audience.
5. It must be comfortable, and allow me to communicate with the audience properly.

Answer:

The seating must encourage good sight lines. The equipment location must be convenient, and keep you or it center stage, depending on the presentation. The room must be a good size and shape, allowing easy communication.

Giving Successful Presentations

Depending on what you need to be featured, you will need to position the equipment appropriately. It should be easy to use but should not obscure or overpower you, the speaker, unless the technology is central.

If you feel audience members should see each other, then the seating will have to be arranged to facilitate that. Arrive early to make sure chairs are arranged in such a way that everyone can see each other.

Any equipment should be positioned so that it's easy and convenient to use. You don't want to trip over wires or traverse the entire room just to hit a button. Make sure it's at hand but not in your way.

If you decide you need to see everyone in the audience, then you need to make sure chairs are arranged to allow that. You may want to arrive early so you can adjust if necessary.

If the room is too small, too large, or awkward, it can be very difficult to communicate well with your audience. You may want to request that the venue be moved to a more fitting location, so arrive early to check it out.

Carlos has just delivered a training lecture. He is reflecting on the room that he used.

Naomi: I'm glad that I asked the training manager to allocate me a larger room than originally planned. We needed a little extra space for when the class broke into groups.

Naomi: Also, that original room was a strange shape, long and thin. It was an interactive session, and it would have been hard for me to pass the products right to the back, or ask people in the back rows for their reactions.

The room that you use has to make it easy for the audience to carry out all of your planned activities. If it is too large, there can be a lack of intimacy. If it is too small, the audience can feel cramped and uncomfortable.

As Carlos recognized, it can be difficult for a presenter to communicate with the whole audience in a long, thin room. The same is true of a very wide room, where you cannot see all of the audience at the same time.

Carlos recently visited his sales department, and gave a talk about the new training modules for the coming year. The sales director allocated Carlos a good-sized meeting room.

Seating

"There were too many chairs, and not enough space, so I removed some chairs. I also rearranged them from classroom style to a horseshoe shape, which provided better sight lines for the audience."

Equipment

"I was mainly talking, and only using the screen occasionally, so I positioned it off to one side. I put the flipchart on the other side, where it was easy to access. I also needed an extension cord--luckily I always carry one in my car."

A horseshoe seating arrangement allows people in a small audience to see each other and the speaker. Classroom-style seating arrangements focus attention on the speaker, but do not allow people to look at each other easily, when they are asking questions.

Placing the viewing screen off-center makes the speaker more prominent. However, if the visual demonstration was the critical part of the presentation, then obviously it would need to be centrally placed to ensure that everyone could see it easily.

Giving Successful Presentations

If you follow the suggestions that you have been shown, you will be better able to control your presentation environment. How successful is the speaker in the next example?

Martin must have had some contact with Youngs Motorcycle Retail in advance of his talk, but he did not check that the allocated room was big enough for his needs. That was his basic mistake. Once he saw the room, he compounded this mistake by not asking to be moved to another one.

If he had been allocated a larger room, all of the engineers could have sat down, and been able to see the demonstration clearly. Control your presentation environment by making sure that you contact the venue in advance. Visit it if possible. Then, arrive early to check that everything is acceptable, because this still gives you time to make changes if necessary.

CHAPTER 2 - DELIVERING THE MESSAGE

CHAPTER 2 - Delivering the Message
  SECTION 1 - Presenting a Positive Image
  SECTION 2 - Structuring Your Presentation
  SECTION 3 - Delivering a Memorable Presentation

SECTION 1 - PRESENTING A POSITIVE IMAGE

SECTION 1 - Presenting a Positive Image

Your audience forms an impression of you very early in your presentation. Where does this image come from? The image you project to your audience is based on what you look like, how you move, and how you speak.

You know the expression: "You never get a second chance to make a first impression"? Well, it's true. So what first impression do you want to give your audience? Your audience members begin to form an impression about you even before you open your mouth to speak. This view is based on what you look like and how you conduct yourself.

Have you ever watched a good speaker and wondered what it is about the way she moves and uses her hands that looks so right and is so effective? The key thing that distinguishes a good speaker is the naturalness of his behavior. He may be talking to dozens or even hundreds of people, but he does not behave as though he is.

Sorin Dumitrascu

Some public speakers feel their voice is not up to the job. This is not true. If you can hold an ordinary conversation, you can project successfully to an audience. It's as simple as that.

PRESENTING A POSITIVE IMAGE

Presenting a positive image

Your audience forms an impression of you very early in your presentation. Where does this image come from? The image you project to your audience is based on what you look like, how you move, and how you speak.

As a speaker, you need to influence each of these factors in a way that ensures your audience is favorably impressed with you, throughout your presentation. Follow along as Sonya and Jeff discuss how impressed they are with the image projected by the speaker they have just listened to.

Sonya: I thought he came across extremely positively.

Jeff: Yes, and as a result, I felt comfortable with him right away. I thought, "Here's a guy who really knows his stuff."

Sonya: I agree, some speakers have a really distracting manner, but I had no difficulty concentrating on this speaker.

Jeff: I implicitly trusted what he was saying to me.

Presenting a positive image to your audience has tremendous benefits. As a result, the audience will:

- relax and feel comfortable in your company,
- be attentive to what you say,
- be likely to trust what you say.

Question

Your colleague is not convinced of the benefits of presenting a positive image to an audience. What do you say to convince her?

Options:

1. "People will be attentive to your presentation."
2. "The audience will feel comfortable with you."
3. "You will require fewer facts to support your arguments."
4. "The audience members are likely to trust what you say to them."
5. "It will increase the strength of your arguments."

Answer:

Presenting a positive image encourages the audience to relax in your company and then listen to and believe your message.

Option 1: This choice is correct. When your colleague presents a positive image, it will be easy for people to pay attention to her. Without a positive image, the speaker may actually distract the audience, so a good image gets good focus.

Option 2: This is a correct choice. When she presents a positive image, people will feel comfortable with her. This means they will listen better to what she is saying and trust her implicitly.

Option 3: This is an incorrect choice. While your colleague may need facts to support her argument, a positive image will help her audience trust her more, which will complement a well-supported presentation.

Option 4: This choice is correct. When people feel comfortable with the speaker, they are more likely to trust what that person is saying more. Your colleague can gain more trust with the audience by presenting a positive image.

Option 5: This is an incorrect choice. The strength of her arguments rests in the facts and examples she uses to support them. However, a positive image does help her audience feel more comfortable with her and trust her more, which will help.

Control the factors that govern your image--your appearance, how you move, and how you speak--and you will get and keep your audience on your side.

CREATING A POSITIVE FIRST IMPRESSION

Creating a positive first impression

You know the expression: "You never get a second chance to make a first impression"? Well, it's true. So what first impression do you want to give your audience?

Your audience members begin to form an impression about you even before you open your mouth to speak. This view is based on what you look like and how you conduct yourself.

The first impression they have of you shapes the way they are likely to respond to your presentation, so you need to do all you can to make sure their impression of you is a good one.

Caroline and Larry formed a poor impression of a speaker as soon as they saw him standing in front of them. Follow along as they discuss their impressions.

Caroline: He looked anxious and unhappy.

Larry: I got the impression he would rather have been somewhere else.

Giving Successful Presentations

Ask yourself: What first impression does your audience want to have? The people you are talking to want you to look:
- in control of yourself and the situation,
- confident in your manner,
- pleased to be there.

You create a positive first impression by meeting the three basic expectations your audience has, right from the beginning.

Question

You are concerned that some of your colleagues don't seem to know how to create a good first impression when they speak in public. What should you say to them?

Options:

1. "You have to come across as highly articulate."

2. "The audience wants you to look pleased to be there speaking to them."

3. "You have to create the impression that you are in control of yourself and the situation."

4. "You must give the audience the idea that your presentation will be entertaining."

5. "You must come across to the audience as being confident."

Answer:

Your audience members want you to come across as in control, confident, and pleased to be there.

Option 1: This choice is incorrect. Regardless of how articulate you are or feel yourself to be, the audience gets their impression from other factors. You create a good first impression by looking happy to be there, confident, and in control.

Option 2: This is a correct choice. If the audience thinks the presenter looks like they would rather be somewhere else, they won't have a good impression of that speaker. Your colleagues should appear happy to be presenting.

Option 3: This choice is correct. When your colleagues give the impression they are in control, the audience will relax and feel comfortable. Your colleagues show control through their dress, stance, and use of hands.

Option 4: This choice is incorrect. A good first impression comes from what you look like and how you conduct yourself. You can create a good first impression by looking happy to be there, confident, and in control.

Option 5: This is a correct choice. If your colleagues appear confident for their presentation, the audience will be comfortable with them. They can display confidence through consistent eye contact. This creates an excellent first impression.

The first thing your audience members want from you is a sense that you are in control. Once they know you are in control, they will begin to relax and listen to you. This is something that Brian understands well. How does he create this initial impression of relaxed control?

clothes

"I make sure I dress appropriately. I don't want to draw negative attention to myself by wearing clothes that are too formal or too informal for the occasion."

stance

"How I stand is really important. I need to be balanced, with my weight evenly distributed between my feet. I always check this before I start speaking. If you're off balance, you look out of control, and it undermines audience confidence."

hands

"What I'm doing with my hands is really important. I either hold them loosely folded in front of me, or I stand with one hand holding my notes and the other at my side."

Speakers who are uncertain and do not feel in control signal this to the audience by an unbalanced stance and by holding their hands stiffly; for example, clasping them behind their backs.

Avoid these negative signals by following Brian's excellent advice.

Caroline and Larry have just come out of another presentation. This time, the speaker created a good impression. As soon as she stood up to speak, they knew that she was brimming with confidence, and really enthusiastic to talk to them.

Brimming with confidence

"From the fact that she made really good, strong eye contact, you could tell she was confident in her ability."

Pleased to be there

"She looked right at us with this very friendly face that seemed to say: 'I'm going to enjoy making this presentation'."

Caroline and Larry's impression that the speaker was a confident person who relished the chance to make her presentation was not an accident. It was the result of positive signals sent by the speaker.

Question

Dawn wants to create a positive first impression on her audience. She knows the three qualities she must communicate in order to do this. However, she does not understand what behaviors she needs to project each quality. Help Dawn by matching each quality to one or more behaviors that she needs to model.

Options:

A. confident

B. in control

C. pleased to be there

Targets:

1. Adopt a balanced stance, with your weight evenly distributed.

2. Dress appropriately for the situation.

3. Maintain a friendly facial expression.

4. Make strong eye contact with the audience.

5. Hold your hands loosely in front of you.

Answer:

If you dress for the occasion, adopt a balanced stance, and hold your hands loosely you create an impression that you are in control. Eye contact projects confidence, and a friendly face says you are pleased to be there.

If you are off balance, then you look out of control. By maintaining a balanced stance, Dawn will convey a sense of being in control. This will make her audience feel more comfortable with her.

By dressing appropriately, she will appear in control, which will draw positive attention. If Dawn dresses too formally or too informally, she will draw negative attention to herself.

If Dawn has a friendly facial expression, then her audience will draw the conclusion she is happy about being there. So if she looks like she's enjoying making the presentation, they will enjoy watching her.

Giving Successful Presentations

Making strong eye contact sends positive signals to the audience, which helps form a good impression. If Dawn looks her audience in the eyes, they will perceive her to be confident about herself and her ability.

If Dawn fidgets or plays with her hands, she will look like she lacks self-control. However, if she holds them loosely in front of her, or uses one to hold her notes, she will give an air of being in control, which creates a good impression.

Lucy was really impressed with the way Tom started his sales presentation yesterday. He had the client on his side even before he'd said a word. Tom's presentation skills have obviously improved a lot--he has not always created such a terrific first impression.

confident

"Before you spoke, you made eye contact with all six people in the room. That was good. You used to look over the heads of the audience, you didn't look confident."

pleased to be there

"You were smiling slightly, and you opened your eyes just a little wider than normal. It made you look warm and approachable. You used to begin with a stiff facial expression. It was actually quite hostile."

in control

"You walked forward and stood still. You only began to move around when you started speaking. You used to rock from foot to foot, or stand with one foot planted in front of the other."

hand gestures

"You kept your hands reasonably still, but you held them in a way that allowed you to easily use gestures once you began to talk. You used to hold your hands stiffly behind your back, or stand at attention, which looked awkward."

clothes

"You were dressed just right for a client presentation. I don't suppose the people in your audience noticed your clothing particularly, but you would have lost them right away if you had looked too casual."

Tom made a good first impression. He was dressed right for a client presentation, stood in a balanced way, avoiding the distracting moving around that used to characterize his presentation. He also held his hands loosely, in a way that did not look awkward, and allowed him to gesture easily. All this communicated to his audience that he was in control.

At the same time, the friendly way he looked at the audience, and the fact that he made eye contact with each person in his small audience, created an anticipation of a pleasurable experience for the people he was talking to.

If Luther had been presenting to the client, he would have worn a suit and tie, but an advertising agency is an informal and youthful environment and he's dressed just right. The fact that he looks friendly will encourage his team to ask questions and promote a cooperative working environment.

You can tell that Luther is basically confident by the direct eye contact he makes with his team, but the fact that he is shifting from foot to foot indicates that he is not totally in control at the start of his presentation. He should be more composed to begin with.

It's not necessary to start speaking as soon as you see the whites of your audience's eyes. Take your time. Use the first few seconds to persuade the audience to like and

Giving Successful Presentations

trust you simply by how you are behaving. They will then be ready to listen appreciatively to your message.

MOVEMENT AND GESTURES

Movement and gestures

Have you ever watched a good speaker and wondered what it is about the way she moves and uses her hands that looks so right and is so effective?

The key thing that distinguishes a good speaker is the naturalness of his behavior. He may be talking to dozens or even hundreds of people, but he does not behave as though he is.

Holly and Joel were very impressed with one speaker at a recent conference they attended, but not with two others. Follow along as they discuss their impressions.

Holly: The first speaker was great. She was very energetic and moved around and gestured a lot, but she looked so natural.

Joel: That's because every time she made a significant movement or gesture, it had a purpose. It wasn't gratuitous.

Joel looks pleased.

Holly: Unlike the second speaker. Watching him was like watching an actor in a play--he looked so fake.

Giving Successful Presentations

Holly looks very critical.

Joel: And that last speaker just stood there with his hands clutching the lectern the whole time. He was so overcontrolled.

Joel looks very critical as well.

Natural-looking movements and gestures:
- have a purpose,
- are not theatrical,
- are not overcontrolled.

You may or may not be animated when you talk informally. That is not important. What is important is that your movements and gestures reflect the real you. Do not adopt a persona when you speak in public.

Question

You have a presentation coming up, and you want to look natural to your audience. How should you behave?

Options:

1. move and gesture as an actor would
2. make sure movements and gestures serve a purpose
3. move with total freedom around the platform
4. avoid theatrical gestures and movements
5. do not overcontrol your movements and gestures

Answer:

In fact, the key to looking natural is making sure that you avoid theatrical gestures or being overcontrolled. The key is to make sure that significant movements and gestures serve a purpose.

Option 1: This choice is incorrect. You want to act naturally. Moving and gesturing like an actor would seem fake and affected to your audience. Act as you normally would, and your audience will feel comfortable with you.

Option 2: This is a correct choice. Any actions or gestures used should be for good reason. When used properly, gestures can emphasize your point but when overused they will seem like false acting and not be received positively.

Option 3: This is an incorrect choice. You want to move naturally, which means a balance between too loose and too controlled. Only move when it helps you make a point and won't seem overly dramatic.

Option 4: This choice is correct. You want your movements to appear natural. Theatrical gestures and movements will seem false, which will turn off your audience. Stick with what feels natural for you.

Option 5: This choice is correct. While on one extreme you don't want to be too theatrical, on the other extreme you shouldn't control yourself excessively. You should appear loose and natural, and your audience will feel comfortable with you.

Warren is a great speaker. He is lively and energetic without being theatrical, and he nearly always succeeds in establishing a close relationship with his audience. Basically, Warren's approach is simple: He behaves in front of an audience as he would in a one-on-one situation.

Purposeful movements and gestures

"I make a lot of small gestures, with an occasional large gesture to emphasize a point. I have a basic standing position, which I move from and then back to as I'm speaking. I move closer to the audience when I want to achieve a greater intimacy."

No theatrical actions

"I don't wave my arms about, stride around the room, or strike postures simply for effect."

No overcontrolling behavior

"I don't stand in the same spot all the time and hide my hands behind my back. Nor do I retreat to the back of the room as though I am trying to hide from the audience."

Most people make small gestures frequently--without being aware of it--as they are speaking. So, not using your hands will only make you seem nervous or unapproachable, which is not what you want! On the other hand, a very big gesture--shaking a fist or waving an open hand or spreading your arms--is very noticeable and should be kept for when you really want to emphasize a point.

When you speak, adopt a basic standing position that is a comfortable distance from your audience. You can then move easily from and back to this position.

When you speak in public, what size is the venue? Large? Small? A variety of sizes? You will find that, to some extent, your movement and gestures will adapt automatically to different venue sizes while still following the same basic rules. In a large auditorium, your gestures and movements will tend to be bigger than in a small room.

Question

Naomi would like to be able to move and gesture naturally in her presentations. She has a general idea of what is required but is not clear how this translates into specific behaviors. What advice do you offer her?

Options:

1. "You should use small gestures freely, but only use big gestures occasionally, for emphasis."

2. "Alternate your gestures by waving your arms and then putting them out of the way."

3. "Stand at a comfortable distance from your audience--one that allows you to easily move toward them."

4. "You ought to adopt a basic standing position that is close to your audience."

5. "Move closer to your audience when you want to achieve greater intimacy."

Answer:

Naomi should gesture freely, but only use large gestures occasionally. She should stand a comfortable distance from her audience, but then move toward them when she wants to increase the psychological intimacy.

Option 1: This is a correct choice. It's natural to make small gestures freely, so Naomi should feel free to do so. She should reserve big gestures for emphasis. This will appear more natural and make her audience feel comfortable with her.

Option 2: This choice is incorrect. Waving arms is a theatrical motion that can seem too unnatural. Naomi should use small gestures as she naturally would and then use larger gestures to emphasize key points.

Option 3: This is a correct choice. Naomi needs a sort of base position that makes her appear in control. However, she should also feel free to move toward the audience when she wants to achieve intimacy.

Option 4: This choice is incorrect. Naomi's basic position should be a comfortable distance from her audience. However, it should also allow her to move closer to them if she feels she needs to. She should soon return to her basic position.

Option 5: This choice is correct. If Naomi's basic position is a good distance, then moving closer will create intimacy without crowding. She can then move back when she needs to re-establish distance.

The way you move and how you use your hands when you present should not be a matter of premeditation or rehearsal--leave that to professional actors. Concentrate on being yourself.

SUCCESSFULLY USE OF YOUR VOICE

Successfully use of your voice

Some public speakers feel their voice is not up to the job. This is not true. If you can hold an ordinary conversation, you can project successfully to an audience. It's as simple as that.

Leroy must speak at a conference this afternoon, and he's worried because his voice does not feel right.

My throat is really constricted, and all the muscles in my face are tight and tense. The audience will be big this afternoon, and I'm afraid that I won't be able to make my voice carry to the back of the hall.

Your voice is a vital instrument, and the anxiety of an impending presentation can place a strain on it. You should not ignore this. On the other hand, you do not generally need to seek specialist help from a voice coach. Nor should you overcompensate by talking too loudly.

To make the most of your voice, you only need to do two things. Before your presentation, take measures to relax your voice. Then, during your presentation, project correctly.

Giving Successful Presentations

Question

You frequently find that before and during a presentation, your voice is tight and uncomfortable.

What should you do?

Options:

1. take measures to relax my voice
2. make sure that I shout loudly so that everyone can hear
3. learn how to project correctly
4. seek assistance from a voice coach
5. accept that the problem is unavoidable

Answer:

You need to take appropriate action to relax your voice and learn how to project properly.

Option 1: This is a correct choice. You need not shout, as that will hurt your voice, but you also don't need to give up entirely. Instead, take measures to relax your voice and you will be able to present without hurting your voice.

Option 2: This is an incorrect choice. If you shout loudly, you will hurt your voice and your listener's ears. Instead, you need to learn how to project correctly, this will carry your voice without straining it.

Option 3: This choice is correct. Having problems with your voice before a presentation is controllable so you don't have to shout at your audience. You can learn how to project your voice without straining it so that everyone can hear you.

Option 4: This choice is incorrect. There is no need to have a voice coach. Two things will help you with this problem and prevent your voice from being strain. First, take measures to relax your voice. Second, learn how to project your voice.

Option 5: This is an incorrect choice. In fact, you can do two things to avoid this problem. You can take measures to relax your voice, and you can project your voice during your presentation.

Rita has developed good vocal habits, so she knows her voice will not let her down even when she's talking to a big audience.

Relax your voice

"I loosen my throat by exercising my voice, and I loosen my face muscles by stretching my lips and tongue and jaw--the body parts you use to articulate."

Project correctly

"I stand straight to encourage good vocal delivery, and I talk, at a volume and intensity that does not cause strain, to the back of the room."

Some speakers try to "save" their voice by talking as little as possible in the hours before their presentation. This is a bad idea. The way to relax your voice is, for the most part, to converse normally. In addition, do some stretching of your articulators to ease tension in your facial muscles. Think of how you stretch muscle groups in your body before sports, and do the same thing with your face.

By standing upright, you will maximize your vocal capacity. By focusing on the need to be audible at the back of the room, you will project so that the sound resonates effortlessly throughout the whole space.

Question

Eugene has asked four of his colleagues for advice about what action he should take to relax his voice and project correctly for his next public speech. Unfortunately, the advice is contradictory. Which suggestion should he act on?

Giving Successful Presentations

Options:
1. "Exercise your articulators, but otherwise rest your voice. Be sure to stand straight when you speak and talk to the back of the room."
2. "You should use your voice for normal conversation in order to exercise it and also stretch your articulators. Stand upright when you speak, and make sure you concentrate on projecting to the back of the room."
3. "Exercise your voice by talking quietly and by stretching your lips and tongue and jaw. Pull your shoulders back when you speak and talk to the people nearest you."
4. "Do not stretch your articulators. Instead, exercise your voice through normal conversation. Make sure you stand up straight when you talk, but avoid projecting consciously to the back of the room."

Answer:
In fact, you will relax your voice by normal conversation coupled with stretching of the lips, tongue, and jaw. If you want to project well, you must stand straight and open your mouth fully.

Option 1: This is an incorrect choice. There is no need for Eugene to rest his voice. To the contrary, by engaging in normal conversation, he will exercise his voice much like stretching muscles before a performance.

Option 2: This is the correct choice. Prior to the presentation, he can exercise his voice in normal conversation. Eugene can also stretch his articulators. During the presentation, standing straight will help him project his voice.

Option 3: This choice is incorrect. Instead of talking quietly, Eugene should talk normally to exercise his voice.

He also can stand up straight, not just pull his shoulders back, and concentrate on projecting to the people at the back of the room.

Option 4: This is an incorrect choice. Eugene should stretch the body parts used to articulate: his lips, tongue, and jaw. Talking normally and standing straight are good tips, but Eugene should project to the back of the room.

So now you know the basic framework you need to adhere to in order to relax your voice and project properly, but how do you apply the lessons in real situations?

Verne has had many years of experience talking to groups large and small, so he's in a good position to pass on his knowledge about the different requirements of voice management.

converse

"Make sure you have opportunities to talk in the hours before a presentation--on the telephone, face to face, or in a business meeting, for example. Have lunch with a colleague you can chat with."

stretch

"Singing is terrific vocal exercise--it really works your vocal range. Try saying tongue twisters or reciting poems or bits from famous speeches that you had to learn at school."

stand straight

"Standing straight does not mean doing anything exaggerated. Just lift your body and your head up and look forward in order to avoid a bent posture that restricts your lung capacity."

articulate

"Concentrate on articulating each sound very clearly by opening your mouth wide and slowing down your speech a little. Imagine that the person farthest from you is a little hard of hearing. A glass of water can help to keep your voice lubricated."

Use your imagination to help you stand correctly. Imagine you are in the military and on parade, with shoulders pushed back and chest stuck out. That's the wrong way to stand!

Now imagine that you are balancing a book on your head. In order to keep the book in position, your weight has to be shifted forward and your knees have to be unlocked. This is the right way to stand straight.

Carlos has occasionally found himself in a venue or situation in which, even with good techniques, he is not able to project adequately.

use a microphone

"If a venue is so large or has such bad acoustics that I can't project adequately without shouting, then I use a microphone."

move closer to the audience

"If the audience members are too distant or I'm outside, I either move so that I'm closer to them or I ask people at the back to move closer."

Under the pressure of the occasion, most speakers tend to start off talking too quickly. To make the most of your vocal resources, you have to give yourself time to sufficiently articulate each consonant and vowel so that you can be heard without effort. This requires you to slow your speech down.

Case Study: Question 1 of 2
Scenario

You are talking to more than 300 marketing managers from all over the world at the Global Brands conference. You have investigated the venue and are reassured that this is a venue with good acoustics. Even so, you are certainly not going to leave anything to chance--you want to be sure that your voice will be audible.

Answer the questions, in order, to show how you will make the most of your voice.

Question

You have a busy schedule, but what will you do before the conference to make sure your voice is in good condition when you make your speech?

Options:

1. spend most of the morning writing a report so that I avoid straining my voice

2. chair the monthly audit meeting as usual

3. go to the large meeting room and practice part of my speech at maximum volume

4. participate in the choir rehearsal the night before I am due to speak

5. reschedule the audit meeting I am due to chair

6. shut my office door and recite a couple of poems I learned at school

Answer

In fact, you should generally use your voice normally before a speaking engagement, so chairing a meeting is a good idea. Your choir rehearsal and poetry recitation will stretch your voice and relax it.

Option 1: This is an incorrect choice. Instead, you will want to speak normally and engage in normal conversation as you otherwise would. This stretches your voice and warms it up for the presentation.

Giving Successful Presentations

Option 2: This is a correct choice. By using your voice as you normally would, you're actually preparing your voice for the presentation. It will help your voice relax so you can deliver a good presentation at the conference.

Option 3: This is an incorrect choice. You want to maintain normal volume prior to the presentation. You shouldn't try to talk too softly or too loudly. Instead, hold normal conversations as you do every day.

Option 4: This is a correct choice. If this is your normal routine, then stick to it. The choir rehearsal will also help you stretch your articulators and help you relax your voice. This will help you deliver your presentation better.

Option 5: This is an incorrect choice. You should go about your normal work and use your voice as you otherwise would. This normal use of your voice will actually help you stretch it and relax it prior to your presentation.

Option 6: This is a correct choice. By reciting the poems at a normal volume, you will help your voice relax. It also helps you stretch your lips, tongue, and jaw for good articulation. This will help you prepare your voice for your presentation.

Case Study: Question 2 of 2

When you get to the hall, you discover it is a multipurpose venue that is used for theater and concerts, as well as conferences. What things should you do to help your vocal projection?

Options:
1. ask the organizers for a microphone
2. articulate each sound very clearly
3. move as close to the audience as possible

4. imagine I am supporting a book or other object on my head

5. bear in mind that there may be people in the audience who do not have perfect hearing

Answer:

You will stand straight if you imagine carrying something on your head. Articulating each sound and remembering that not everyone has perfect hearing will help you to project to the back.

Option 1: This is an incorrect choice. Since it is used for plays and conferences as well as concerts, the acoustics are probably really good. You probably will not need a microphone, but you will need to articulate very clearly.

Option 2: This is a correct choice. You will want to open your mouth wide and slow down your speed a little. Take time to articulate each consonant and vowel so that you can be heard without effort.

Option 3: This is an incorrect choice. If you were in a more difficult venue, you might consider this action. However, you'll be presenting in a venue made for good acoustics. You'll simply need to project well.

Option 4: This is a correct choice. You will want to stand up straight and have good posture. This does not mean pushing your shoulders back and chest out. Imagining a book on your head keeps your knees bent and weight shifted forward.

Option 5: This is a correct choice. In fact, to help your voice projection, imagine somebody on the very back row is a little hard of hearing. Keeping this in mind will help you project well.

Take the right actions to make the most of your voice. Speaking at normal business meetings will provide good exercise, and will relax your voice. So too will singing at choir rehearsal and reciting poetry, both of which will help by stretching your articulators. You will achieve good projection by standing upright, as though you had an object balanced on your head, and articulating each sound clearly. It will aid projection to bear in mind that there may well be people in your audience whose hearing is less than perfect.

Remember, your voice will enhance your image as a competent speaker provided you do the simple things required to relax and project it correctly.

SECTION 2 - STRUCTURING YOUR PRESENTATION

SECTION 2 - Structuring Your Presentation

You have to follow through on the time and effort you have spent preparing your presentation. When you get face-to-face with your audience, you need to communicate the structure of your talk with the utmost clarity.

Three parts of your presentation are particularly important for communicating the structure. You need:

- a strong start phase to establish your agenda,
- a clearly organized development phase,
- a strong, emphatic ending.

The first few minutes of your presentation are vital. We can all think of speakers who started badly and went downhill from there.

You need a strong start. This means capturing and holding the attention of your audience. Get the people in your audience interested from the start, and they are likely to stay with you. Lose them now, and you've probably lost them for good. So how do you make a strong start? The first few minutes of this speaker's presentation were terrific, but look at the situation 15 minutes later. What happened?

This speaker assumed that because the audience members were initially interested in what she was saying, they would keep paying attention. Don't make this mistake. Her presentation lacked a clear development, so she lost her audience. Remember, a speaker is competing for attention with other subjects or concerns that might enter each person's mind. Also, there is a tendency for concentration levels to decline after the first ten minutes or so.

The final impression that you leave in your audience members' minds will remain the longest. That's why the ending of your presentation is so important.

THE STRUCTURE OF YOUR PRESENTATION

The structure of your presentation

You have to follow through on the time and effort you have spent preparing your presentation. When you get face-to-face with your audience, you need to communicate the structure of your talk with the utmost clarity.

Three parts of your presentation are particularly important for communicating the structure. You need:
- a strong start phase to establish your agenda,
- a clearly organized development phase,
- a strong, emphatic ending.

Chad is very popular with his audiences. One reason for this is because he always communicates the structure of his talks clearly.

reinforces messages

"The fact that the structure was so well communicated helped to reinforce his key messages--they really stood out."

enhances concentration

Giving Successful Presentations

"I find I can concentrate longer because Chad communicates the structure of his presentation so clearly."

assists memory

"I remembered the key messages of Chad's presentation once it was over."

Communicating your structure clearly does not mean that your audience will like the message of your presentation or trust it. However, it will guarantee that your key messages will be delivered more forcefully, your audience will concentrate longer, and people will remember your key messages once the presentation is over.

Question

You have a colleague who will soon make her first presentation. You want to explain to her the benefits of making sure that she communicates the structure clearly to her audience. What do you say?

Options:

1. "It will help the audience to concentrate longer."

2. "Your main messages will be delivered more forcefully."

3. "The audience will approve of what you have to say."

4. "The audience will remember your message after the presentation is over."

5. "You will be believed by your audience."

Answer:

Communicating a clear structure is important because it will reinforce your messages and help their retention. It will also mean that the audience can concentrate for longer.

Option 1: This is a correct choice. When audience members know what a presentation will cover and where it's headed, they can concentrate better and longer. By providing structure, your colleague will improve audience concentration.

Option 2: This is a correct choice. When the structure is communicated clearly, it reinforces the content. This helps your colleague's audience focus on what her key messages are.

Option 3: This is an incorrect choice. Good structure does not mean her audience will like what she has to say. It does mean, however, that they can concentrate on it and will remember it, and that her points will be delivered more forcefully.

Option 4: This is a correct choice. A good structure that is clearly articulated will help her audience remember the main points. They can recall these more easily because they were clear and stood out.

Option 5: Incorrect. Good structure does not mean the audience will automatically trust the content. It will guarantee that your colleague's key messages are delivered better, the audience will concentrate longer and will remember key points.

Help the audience by making the structure of your presentation obvious. Get off to a strong start, organize the development clearly, and deliver a strong ending.

KEY ELEMENTS OF A STRONG PRESENTATION OPENING

Key elements of a strong presentation opening

The first few minutes of your presentation are vital. We can all think of speakers who started badly and went downhill from there.

You need a strong start. This means capturing and holding the attention of your audience. Get the people in your audience interested from the start, and they are likely to stay with you. Lose them now, and you've probably lost them for good. So how do you make a strong start?

Opal has been making dynamic presentations for years as part of the sales team for Tux Confectionery, and nobody needs to tell her about the need for an attention-grabbing opening.

use positive language

"I have to express myself using words and phrases that are distinctly positive and that will indicate my strong commitment to my presentation and to the audience."

provide a hook

"I make a remark that will intrigue and interest the audience members and act as a 'hook' for their attention so that they want to hear more."

tell the audience the structure

"I always make sure that I satisfy the audience's natural curiosity by indicating the structure of the presentation, so everyone knows what I'm going to cover."

To capture the interest of your audience members from the very beginning, you must:
- use positive language,
- provide a hook,
- tell the audience the structure of the presentation.

Question

Todd knows that if he can just get the first couple of minutes of his presentation right, it will probably be a success.

What should he do during this time?

Options:

1. He should avoid speaking and show a slide instead.
2. Todd should say something to hook the attention of his audience.
3. He should choose positive words and phrases.
4. Todd should tell a long personal story.
5. He should indicate the structure of his presentation.

Answer:

Todd should indicate the structure of his presentation, use positive language, and say something to "hook" the audience's attention in order to get off to a strong start.

Option 1: This is an incorrect choice. Todd can begin the presentation by saying something to gain the audiences attention. He should use positive language, use a hook to grab their attention, and tell the audience what the structure will be.

Option 2: This is a correct choice Todd can begin with a remark or figure that will grab the interest of his audience. That will "hook" his audience into listening to what he has to say.

Option 3: This choice is correct. By choosing words that convey a positive attitude, Todd will convey a sense of commitment to his presentation and his audience.

Option 4: This is an incorrect choice. Todd will want to hook his audience quickly. He should begin with positive language and use a specific hook to capture their interest. Todd should also state the structure of his presentation.

Option 5: This choice is correct. By covering the structure, Todd will satisfy his audience's curiosity. The audience will know what to expect and will be able to follow along better.

Noah captures his audience's attention when he starts speaking, but not in the right way.

I'd like to start by saying that I'm the world's leading expert on this subject.

I'm going to talk for about a half an hour about my research this year. You'll find out what I have to say as I go along, so just relax and listen.

Saying he's the world's leading expert will act as a hook, and his language as he sings his own praises is positive, but Noah's arrogant start will, of book, alienate his audience. Also, merely saying that he's going to talk about his research doesn't meet his audience's need to be told the presentation structure.

So what would be a better way to behave?

Trudy is a widely admired presenter and has some excellent strategies for immediately engaging her audience.

use positive language

"I often say something to praise or flatter the audience members. For example, I tell them how much I respect their knowledge. Also, I use inclusive pronouns, such as 'we' or 'us,' to promote the idea of my working positively with the audience."

provide a hook

"Using a startling fact or figure is a great way to make people sit up and take notice. Opening with a short, relevant anecdote has the same effect."

tell the audience the structure

"I provide the audience with a road map. I either list all the main points I will cover or just mention where I will start and where I expect to go by the end of my presentation."

Praise and flattery are positive, but they have to be genuine. If you say, "I know how busy you all are, and I really appreciate your taking the time to let me talk to you," or "My colleague Eddy, who spoke to you last year, told me about your insightful questions, and I really look forward to hearing your reaction when I've finished my presentation," then you must mean it, or your audience will know at once.

Your presentation road map should not have every little detail on it, but a single slide listing your key points is a good way to open and gives you the chance to touch briefly on some of your main messages.

Imogene, the CEO of Lokon Components, is making a presentation to senior managers at Deer Elektrics, with whom she has every hope of agreeing on a mutually beneficial joint venture. During her opening, she succeeds in capturing and holding her audience.

Use positive language

"I am confident that we can solve these issues together. This presentation and our discussions after it will, I believe, provide us with a way forward."

Provide a hook

"The trends and the numbers are unequivocal. We can double turnover and more than double profit after tax in the next two fiscal years."

Tell the audience the structure

"To start with, I need to compare figures in the three markets. Then I want to outline the exciting opportunities I see. Finally, I'll focus on exactly how we can realize those opportunities together."

Question

Esther is impressed with Reuben's recent presentations. As she tells you, he has done a number of things early on which have set him on the right track.

Match each requirement of a strong presentation opening with the corresponding behavior described by Esther.

Options:

A. positive language
B. a hook
C. indication of the structure

Targets:

1. "Reuben used attention-grabbing facts or figures."
2. "He told a short, relevant story early on."
3. "He said he was impressed with his audience's accomplishments."

4. "Reuben listed key points and where the presentation would start and end."

5. "He employed inclusive pronouns such as 'we' and 'us'."

Answer:

Startling facts and figures and anecdotes "hook" an audience, praise and flattery and inclusive pronouns are positive, and you need to indicate the structure through listing key content or where the presentation will begin and end.

By grabbing attention with facts or figures, Reuben was using a hook for his audience. This is a good way to get and hold their interest, as it apparently did for Esther.

A hook can take the form of a short, anecdotal story at the beginning of the presentation. By telling a short, but relevant, story, Reuben grabbed his audience's attention.

If done genuinely, Reuben's flattery of the audience will help him connect with the audience instead of alienate them. He needs to show respect for their knowledge as well. However, this must be a genuine statement.

By listing the key start and end points of his presentation, Reuben communicated structure early on. This provided his audience with a road map of the main points that would be covered.

Using inclusive pronouns is a way of connecting with the audience through positive language. Instead of establishing a "me" versus "them," inclusive pronouns promote the idea that Reuben is working collaboratively with the audience.

Your opening remarks should provide a strong platform on which you can develop the rest of your speech. The

Giving Successful Presentations

first moments of your presentation are vital, so work hard to capture and hold your audience's attention.

SIGNALING THE DEVELOPMENT OF THE MAIN POINTS

Signaling the development of the main points
The first few minutes of this speaker's presentation were terrific, but look at the situation 15 minutes later. What happened?

This speaker assumed that because the audience members were initially interested in what she was saying, they would keep paying attention. Don't make this mistake. Her presentation lacked a clear development, so she lost her audience. Remember, a speaker is competing for attention with other subjects or concerns that might enter each person's mind. Also, there is a tendency for concentration levels to decline after the first ten minutes or so.

As a speaker, you have to encourage and enable the audience to retain high concentration throughout by developing the content of your presentation with crystal clarity. You do this by strongly signaling:
- the end of each key point,
- the start of each new point,

Giving Successful Presentations

- the connection between points.

Your presentation is organized around its main points; they are the essential elements of the story you are telling. When these points and the connections between them are powerfully communicated to your audience, they command attention. Your story will have a clear development.

Question

You are concerned about the development phase of your talks. Ryan, a more experienced colleague, tells you how to achieve a clear development.

Which pieces of advice from Ryan do you accept?

Options:

1. "Signal the connection between your anecdotes."

2. "Communicate the end of each main point strongly."

3. "Indicate several times how long your presentation will last."

4. "Signal the connection between the key points in your story."

5. "Indicate the start of every new point."

Answer:

The development of your presentation will be clear if you emphatically signal the start and the end of each key point and also make a connection between the points.

Option 1: This choice is incorrect. You will want to signal the connection between key points, not between anecdotes. Doing so will command attention and help the audience retain concentration.

Option 2: This is a correct choice. You will want to emphasize the end of each key point strongly. This will help your audience retain their concentration as they see the content of the presentation unfolding with precise clarity.

Option 3: This is an incorrect choice. Giving the length of your presentation will not help your audience concentrate longer. Instead, you should communicate the end of each main point, the start of each point, and the connections between them.

Option 4: This choice is correct. Your entire presentation is a story you are telling. You will want to signal how the key points are connected. This helps the story develop clearly for your audience.

Option 5: This is a correct choice. As the presenter, you have to encourage your audience to keep their attention on you. You do this by communicating the start of a new point clearly. This helps your audience see how your presentation is unfolding.

Building the relationship between the parts of your story is a function of how you signal. But what signals are unmistakable to your audience?

Trudy is about to make a sales presentation with a big account riding on it, so it's really important to her that the client concentrates as she expands on her opening remarks.

silence

"When I come to the end of each part of my pitch, I'll stop talking for a moment to let the client absorb what I've said."

language

"I'm going to use specific words and phrases as a way of signaling the end of one section, the start of another, or to indicate the connection between them."

tempo

Giving Successful Presentations

"I intend to noticeably change my speed of delivery as a way of commanding attention at important points."

Trudy's approach is a good one that you should follow. She holds her audience's hand and guides people through her presentation. The fact that she uses a combination of deliberate signals at key turning points will ensure that her listeners always know what is important and are never lost.

Spontaneity has its place in a presentation when it comes to the details of what you say. But shifting from one section of your presentation to another is too important to leave to chance. You should plan exactly how you are going to signal the main points.

Question

You are explaining to your assistant, Kevin, who is new to presentations, the kind of signals he can use to consciously indicate the main points in his presentation narrative. What do you say to him?

Options:

1. "Ask your audience to split into breakout groups."
2. "You should use silence as a signaling device."
3. "Catch the audience's attention by telling a joke."
4. "Choose particular words or phrases to indicate the end of one section, the start of another, or the connection between sections."
5. "You should start pacing rapidly around the floor."
6. "Alter the speed at which you are talking enough for the audience to notice."

Answer:

The way to indicate the development points in a presentation is through the use of silence, words and phrases that act as signals, and by changing the speed at which you speak.

Option 1: This is an incorrect choice. To indicate his main points, Kevin can use silence, certain language patterns, and tempo. These signals will cue the audience to the main points. Breaking them into groups will not.

Option 2: This is a correct choice. When Kevin comes to the end of a point, he can use silence to signal that end. This silent space lets the audience absorb what he has said and signals that he is moving to a new point.

Option 3: This choice is incorrect. Telling jokes will not send any sort of signal to the audience. However, Kevin can use silence, change the tempo of his speaking, or use key words as signals during his presentation.

Option 4: This is a correct choice. If Kevin uses certain words to indicate the end or start of a new point, the audience will recognize that pattern. This will help them follow the presentation and keep their concentration.

Option 5: This is an incorrect choice. Doing so will look like Kevin has lost control of the present. To keep the audience focused, he should use signals like certain words as indicators, use silence, and change his tempo.

Option 6: This is a correct choice. A change in tempo will catch the audience's attention. By changing his speed, Kevin can help the audience take note of his key points.

Try to recall the last really good presentation you saw. The speaker most likely made use of such techniques as intense quiet moments, changes of tempo, and turns of phrase to signal when the presentation changed direction.

silence

Use silence to signal the end of a point. A silence of five seconds is acceptable. Look away from your audience at the same time to emphasize the break between the points. At the end of the silence, bring up your next visual to indicate a new part of your presentation.

language

A phrase like, "The last thing I want to say about this year is..." or, "That's all I want to say about..." signals the end of a section. Single words like "OK" or "now" can signal a new point. Or introduce a new point directly by saying something like, "Now we need to look at..."

tempo

When you suddenly start to speak more slowly or more rapidly than normal, the audience will notice. You can use markedly rapid or slow speech to signal the end of one section or the start of a new one.

Dave and Michelle use language to make a connection between key points in their presentations. They make remarks that refer back to a previous section or forward to a new one.

Refer forward

"I'll say, 'I'm going to move on to next year's budget in just a moment' or 'Next we'll look at how the results have been transformed.'"

Refer back

"I'll say, 'As I told you in the first part of my talk...' or, 'As I said earlier....'"

Elliott is the project manager responsible for the construction of a new shopping mall. He has to brief the client on progress. Elliott is thinking about how to develop the part of his presentation that delays with delays, and how he plans to overcome them.

End of the section on delays

"I'll detail the different delays, and then I'll speak more slowly and say something like, 'OK, I've said enough about the delays, but as I will show you in the next part of my presentation, we can catch up by the end of next month.'"

Between the two sections

"I'll stop and look down at my computer screen and maybe take a drink of water before going on."

Start of the section dealing with next month's schedule

"I'll begin by saying, 'Well, now let's look at the actions I've put in place so that we will overcome the delays by June 30th at the latest.'"

Elliott is going to do a great job of sewing his presentation together. He intends to signal to the audience that he is about to finish with the section dealing with delays, both by language and by a change of tempo. His silence while he looks down at his computer screen indicates the end of the section even more emphatically, and at the same time he links to the next section. By saying "As I will show you in the next part of my presentation...," he makes a connection between the two points.

The single word "well..." will strongly signal the beginning of the next section, and the rest of his remark provides an introduction to the content of the section.

Irma does a reasonably good job of developing the two sections of her presentation. She indicates clearly in words when one section is coming to an end, and she provides a verbal introduction at the start of the next one. She also uses silence effectively to underscore the end of the section on quality issues.

However, tempo is an effective signaling device that she does not think of exploiting, and she does not make an explicit connection between the two parts of her presentation. As a speaker, you have to deal with the realities of your situation. The people in your audience have other things going on in their lives to distract them from your presentation. To keep them concentrating, you have to signal the parts of the story as clearly as possible.

Or to put it another way: Be listener-friendly!

A STRONG PRESENTATION ENDING

A strong presentation ending
The final impression that you leave in your audience members' minds will remain the longest. That's why the ending of your presentation is so important.

Ajay delivers many major conference speeches, and he always works really hard to deliver a powerful ending.

Remember
"The people in the audience will forget much of what you tell them, but they will remember your last remarks."

Message
"Your ending is your last chance to make sure people remember the most important part of your message."

By the time you approach the end of your presentation, your audience has become accustomed to your voice and delivery, and no matter how well you are doing, it is harder to keep people concentrating on you than it was at the start. A strong ending means regaining audience attention by:

- focusing attention on you, as the presenter,
- concentrating attention on your message.

Giving Successful Presentations

A question-and-answer session will probably keep the audience interested and engaged, but it will remove you and your message from the center of the stage. A question-and-answer session can be a valuable part of a presentation, but it is not a way to achieve a strong ending.

Question

Your colleague Douglas is quite pleased with most parts of his presentations, but he would like the endings to be strong. He asks your advice.

What do you say to him?

Options:

1. "A strong ending requires bright and well-designed slides."

2. "To achieve a strong ending, you must concentrate audience attention on you, the speaker."

3. "To end strongly, you must lead a question-and-answer session."

4. "A strong ending comes from focusing the audience on your message."

5. "You will finish strongly if you keep your presentation as short as possible."

Answer:

For an ending to be strong, attention must be fully focused on the speaker and the message.

Option 1: This is an incorrect choice. Douglas needs to focus his audience on him as the presenter and on his message. Bright, well-designed slides will not necessarily help him achieve that end.

Option 2: This is a correct choice. Audience attention should be returned to Douglas, by the end, they will be used to him and how he speaks. Douglas needs to keep himself at center stage so the audience will remember him.

Option 3: This choice is incorrect. While a question-and-answer session may be a good part of a presentation, it is a weak ending. It does not leave the audience focused on Douglas or his message.

Option 4: This is a correct choice. Douglas needs to end with his audience thinking about his message. The ending is his last opportunity to make sure he emphasizes his key points.

Option 5: This is an incorrect choice. Douglas needs to end by keeping his audience focused on him and his message. This may or may not take a short amount of time, so Douglas should take what he needs to end strongly.

Follow along as Hilary and Mark discuss the best way to refocus audience attention on themselves at the end of a talk.

Hilary: Most of the time when I'm presenting, I'm quite spontaneous. I let myself move around freely. But I really control my movements as I approach the end of my presentation.

Mark: Me too. It's a good way to regain total audience attention.

Hilary: What about your voice?

Mark: Yes, I also make sure I'm aware of how the words are coming out of my mouth. I work hard to control my voice.

You have been presenting in a certain way, in a style that you are comfortable with, for maybe 15 or 20 minutes. Then you reach the final phase of your talk. The

first thing you need to do is make the audience sit up and take notice by changing your style of delivery. Do this by:
- controlling your movements,
- controlling your voice.
- Follow along to learn what Mark and Hilary do to make sure their audience notices their final words.

Mark: I believe in the old adage, "Tell them what you've told them." The audience needs to be reminded of what you've discussed.

Hilary: Right, but you also need to end on a forward-looking, positive note, so people leave the room with a spring in their step.

A summary is part of a strong ending. It is a way to ensure that each person leaves the room remembering what you want him or her to remember.

Usually you do not want the people in your audience to be passive receivers of your message. Ending on a positive note is a tool that encourages people to translate the message into action.

Question

Peg has been watching speakers to learn from how they behave at the final phase of their presentations. She tells you what she has seen.

Which behaviors that she describes should she copy?

Options:

1. "The speaker reminded us of what he'd already told us."

2. "The speaker began to move about wildly."

3. "He ended on an upbeat note, with a focus on the future."

4. "I noticed that she began to control her movements more."

5. "She repeated everything she had said once more."

6. "He seemed to know exactly what he was doing with his voice."

Answer:

A positive ending requires the speaker to be in control of his or her voice and movements, to summarize content, and to end on a positive note.

Option 1: This choice is correct. A good rule of thumb is to tell them what you've already told them. If Peg does this in her presentations, she will help her audience remember what they have discussed.

Option 2: This choice is incorrect. Peg should become more controlled at the end of her presentation. By doing so, the audience will sit up and take notice that she is being serious. She regains control of the presentation to end on a positive note.

Option 3: This is a correct choice. Peg should end her presentation on an upbeat note as well. While she should wrap up what she's covered, Peg can also encourage them to take some sort of action in the future.

Option 4: This is a correct choice. People notice when a speaker starts controlling her movements more. Peg can also do this to catch her audience's attention at the end of her presentation to focus on what she wants.

Option 5: This is an incorrect choice. While Peg does want to remind them of what she's covered, she shouldn't repeat everything again. Peg can simply remind them of the highlights and end on an upbeat note that encourages action.

Option 6: This is a correct choice. Peg can regain attention at the end of her presentations by controlling her voice. When she controls her voice, she can change her delivery style, which will cause the audience to take notice.

The techniques you use to modify your delivery style for the final part of your presentation can be applied in different ways. Remember that you're only interested in the end result, directing 100% of the audience's attention on you and your words.

Control your movement

Move around less than usual or stand in one place. This will concentrate attention on you. At the same time, link any noticeable gestures to your words; for example, by counting the points you make on your fingers.

Control your voice

Make your audience concentrate by speaking more emphatically, stressing each important word and phrase.

Summarize

In a technical presentation, you may need to summarize in detail with the aid of slides. In other presentations, a short, punchy summary in a few sentences may be better. Summarize in a sentence starting like this: "I want you to remember...."

End on a positive note

You can encapsulate a positive note into a quotation. Be forward-looking. For example, predict success or tell the audience members how you want them to translate the message of your presentation into action.

A single visual with a few bullet points will be sufficient to support his summarizing remarks for this nonspecialist audience. The final thing he needs to do is to look forward. Reminding people that the finance department is a resource they can use, will work well.

Case Study: Question 1 of 2

Scenario

You work for Eagle Air. You are giving a talk, supported by much data, about recruitment trends in your company to fellow human resources professionals at the "HR Now" conference. You have been speaking for 35 minutes, and you have another five to go.

Answer the questions, in order, to show how you will bring your presentation to a close.

Question

You have put a lot of energy into communicating the trends you see. You now want to make sure that you behave in a way that gives your presentation a strong ending. What do you do?

Options:

1. I quickly and loudly make my final three remarks, using a variety of interesting gestures.

2. Instead of moving around so much, I stand in one place.

3. As I make each of my final three remarks, I speak very quietly, so that I am difficult to hear.

4. As I make each of my final three remarks about the trends, I point directly to the supporting visual, speaking emphatically as I do.

5. I move around more than I have been doing and increase the volume at which I speak.

6. As I make my final points, I articulate each one.

Answer:

To maximize audience attention, you should stand in one place or move around less, but gesture to support your points and speak emphatically.

Option 1: This choice is incorrect. Every aspect of what you do at the end should be controlled. You should stay still to get attention focused on you. Gestures should emphasize what you are saying, and your voice should be controlled but emphatic.

Option 2: This is a correct choice. When you stand in one place, people will directly focus on you, especially if you've been moving around. By stopping, you will catch their attention and get the audience concentrating on you.

Option 3: This is an incorrect choice. Instead of speaking quietly, you should speak more emphatically. You do this by stressing each important word and phrase. Such voice control will help your audience concentrate better.

Option 4: This is a correct choice. By doing so, you link your gestures to important words. You also make good use of the slides for summarizing and help the audience remember what you've covered.

Option 5: This is an incorrect choice. You want to demonstrate control over your movements and voice. A stronger way to end is to stand in one place and speak emphatically. Use your words and motions to direct attention, not lose it.

Option 6: This is a correct choice. You will want your words and tone to be precise so the audience understands you clearly. An emphatic tone will get their attention and focus them. Clear articulation aids their concentration.

Case Study: Question 2 of 2

What do you say at the end of your presentation to impress your message on the minds of your audience members?

Options:

1. "Let me remind you briefly of the key trends that I've described in detail. Take a look at this slide."

2. "I want to finish by giving you some more detail about the trend toward short-term contracts that I mentioned earlier."

3. "Let me finish with a joke I heard this morning about the problems of parenthood."

4. "There's a little-known but uplifting and relevant remark by Franklin D. Roosevelt that I'd like to leave you with..."

5. "Altogether, it's clear that the trends we can see are not a reason for fear; they're a way of guaranteeing our long-term future."

Answer:

You need to summarize with the aid of at least one visual for this specialist audience, and then end on a positive note; a positive remark or quotation can achieve this.

Option 1: This is a correct choice. This is an effective way to summarize your presentation. Furthermore, by using a supporting slide and tying gestures to words, you are controlling your movements for added emphasis.

Option 2: This is an incorrect choice. The end of your presentation is not a time to be providing more detail about one point. Instead, concentrate on summarizing your presentation and emphasize the main points.

Option 3: This is an incorrect choice. The topic of parenthood in no way relates to your presentation. You need to end with a summary that ties back into what you've covered, hitting the high points the audience should remember.

Option 4: This is a correct choice. As long as the quote is relevant, this is an excellent way to end the presentation. This will end your presentation on a positive

Giving Successful Presentations

note but also underscore everything you've said during your presentation.

Option 5: This is a correct choice. This statement ends with a positive note. You want to leave your audience on this note, possibly encouraging them to take action. This will help them remember your message and even do something about it.

Standing in one place in the final phase of your presentation is good because it will encourage the audience to focus on your words. Your presentation included much data, and you will require more than a few sentences and visual support to summarize.

If your quotation is short as well as relevant, it will leave a positive impression and be a good lead-in to your final, forward-looking comment.

A strong ending is the best tool you have in your toolbox to ensure the long-term success of your presentation. It will help you to ensure that your audience members remember and act on what you have told them.

SECTION 3 - DELIVERING A MEMORABLE PRESENTATION

SECTION 3 - Delivering a Memorable Presentation

Many of the presentations you've sat through have probably been adequate. Some may have been inadequate. A few, probably very few, have possessed that "wow factor" that made them truly memorable.

We are all unique, and everyone has his or her own basic delivery style with which he or she is comfortable. Your basic style is the style you use in ordinary conversation, for example. But a normal conversation is a dialogue, and the necessary variety is provided by, or stimulated by, the other person or people you are talking to.

In a presentation, you have to generate the variety yourself to make sure that your delivery does not become monotonous. Your presentation needs to have high-energy periods. It also needs more relaxed, lower-energy periods.

Giving Successful Presentations

Most people are outgoing. Generally speaking, when they come into contact with other people, they want to form some kind of relationship, and this is as true in a presentation situation as in any other form of interaction. One of the "wow factors" that makes a presentation special is the speaker, simply through the language that he or she uses, encouraging and developing a relationship with the audience.

Make a list of the top five movies you've seen. What makes them so great? Are there any lessons you can learn from them and apply to make your presentations memorable? If you're watching a movie on television and you're not enjoying it, you change channels or turn it off. If you go to a movie theater and the film bores you, you take your revenge by warning your friends not to go.

DELIVERING A MEMORABLE PRESENTATION

Delivering a memorable presentation

Many of the presentations you've sat through have probably been adequate. Some may have been inadequate. A few, probably very few, have possessed that "wow factor" that made them truly memorable.

But there is no mystery to giving your presentation the stamp of true quality. Roger presents seminars for business leaders and is renowned as a wonderful public speaker. Early in his speaking career, Roger noticed how poor speakers behave, and he has based his success as a speaker on using strategies that do the opposite.

interact

"I always interact a lot with the audience--partly through what I say to people and

partly through how I behave. Bad speakers ignore the audience most of the time-- they could be talking to an empty room."

vary content

Giving Successful Presentations

"I vary the content in my presentations. Variety is really important. In a bad presentation, the content and how it is delivered are all too similar."

energize

"I keep the energy level high most of the time when I'm talking. A lot of speakers are dull and lack energy."

The relationship Roger develops with his audience helps him when he meets them one-on-one. He also believes that his reputation for business excellence is due partly to the quality of his speeches.

There are practical benefits to being able to deliver a presentation that can make an audience let out a collective "Wow!"

- The speaker is associated with excellence.
- It helps to promote long-term business relationships.
- It helps to "sell" the message of the presentation.

Of book, knowing how to make your presentation special does not absolve you of the need to prepare thoroughly. And no matter how good a speaker you are, all audiences have a limited concentration span.

Question

Some of your colleagues think that "good enough" is OK when it comes to presentations. You are going to send them an e-mail stating the benefits of knowing how to make a memorable presentation. What points do you make?

Options:

1. It will enable the audience to listen for much longer.
2. It helps to build long-term business relationships.
3. It associates you with the concept of excellence.

4. The audience is more likely to buy the presentation message.

5. You will spend less time organizing your presentation.

Answer:

Being able to deliver a presentation with the wow factor helps business relationships, associates you with excellence, and makes you more likely to sell your presentation idea to the audience.

Option 1: This is an incorrect choice. All audiences have a limited concentration span. You should emphasize that having a memorable presentation makes the best use of the time given and helps the audience remember the content better.

Option 2: This choice is correct. When you meet with clients one-on-one after a presentation, a memorable presentation can help your colleagues build strong relationships. It develops a good reputation from the start.

Option 3: This is a correct choice. If your colleagues give memorable speeches, they will develop a reputation for excellence. That reputation will follow them into smaller settings where they may find it easier to develop client relationships.

Option 4: This is a correct choice. If the audience is wowed by your presentation, they are more likely to remember it. Part of the message is your colleagues' delivery, so a memorable delivery will enhance the message.

Option 5: This is an incorrect choice. Your colleagues will still need to spend adequate time preparing for their presentations. Thorough preparation is a perfect counterpart to knowing how to make that presentation dazzle.

Aim for more than mere competence. Give your presentation the wow factor by observing excellent speakers at work and following their examples.

TECHNIQUES USED TO ACHIEVE VARIETY

Techniques used to achieve variety

Variety makes things more interesting. It's as true of a presentation as anything else. Without variety, your presentation will be tedious.

Barbara: It was just one fact after another, long lists of information. Does he seriously expect us to remember them?

Karen: And so boring to listen to. He went on and on in the same monotonous way.

Mike's presentation lacked variety. The material was all the same, and it was delivered in the same way. No wonder Barbara and Karen were bored. All successful presentations contain:
- different kinds of content,
- a variety of delivery styles.

Constant variety of content and delivery style means that audience interest and excitement is always maintained. People are eager to know what's coming next.

Question

Giving Successful Presentations

You have a presentation to make tomorrow. How will you introduce variety?

Options:

1. introduce different kinds of content
2. use a mixture of delivery styles
3. change your clothing halfway through
4. vary the presentation objective

Answer:

A presentation that maintains audience interest by having variety uses a mix of delivery styles and content.

Option 1: This is a correct choice. You can introduce variety by mixing up the types of content. Instead of only having statements, you can use questions, facts and case studies to liven up your presentation.

Option 2: This is a correct choice. Varying your style is a great way of improving your presentation. You can have a more excited style for moments of high energy, but a reserved style when you want the audience to be more reflective.

Option 3: This is an incorrect choice. This is impractical and is not the sort of variety an audience is looking for. Rather you can vary your content and your style throughout. This will keep your audience interested.

Option 4: This choice is incorrect. Your presentation objective remains the same. However, you can vary your style and your content throughout to help you better achieve that objective. Variety will keep your audience better engaged.

We are all unique, and everyone has his or her own basic delivery style with which he or she is comfortable. Your basic style is the style you use in ordinary conversation, for example. But a normal conversation is a dialogue, and the necessary variety is provided by, or stimulated by, the other person or people you are talking to.

In a presentation, you have to generate the variety yourself to make sure that your delivery does not become monotonous. Your presentation needs to have high-energy periods. It also needs more relaxed, lower-energy periods.

High-energy moments generate excitement. Lower-energy moments help the audience to reflect on something you've said.

Virginia is a project leader for Bio Technology Research. At the end of every project, she has to prepare a report and present her findings, and it's important that she does not overwhelm the client by simply talking about pages of research data that are already in the report.

facts

"I provide and discuss groups of facts. They are important, but they are only one part of the content, and I always use the bare minimum."

statements and questions

"I make general statements and ask questions. These are important kinds of content."

case studies

"In each main section, I use at least one case study, sometimes detailed and long, sometimes quite brief."

Make sure that your presentations always strike a balance between the three types of content: groups of facts, statements and questions, and case studies.

Question

Giving Successful Presentations

What should you say to your colleague Ross to enable him to introduce variety into the presentation he has to make tomorrow?

Options:

1. "Present groups of facts in your presentation and talk about them, but no more than necessary."

2. "Use lots of case studies and very few facts in your presentation."

3. "Include intense moments in your presentation, as well as more relaxed periods."

4. "Ask questions, and also make general statements."

5. "Make sure most of your presentation is a detailed discussion of facts."

6. "Include case studies of different lengths. Make sure each part of your presentation has at least one."

Answer:

A presentation must have periods of high and low intensity. It needs a variety of case studies, questions and statements, and groups of facts, but minimal time should be spent on the facts.

Option 1: This is a correct choice. It is a good idea to include facts; they're an important part of the content. However, they should be used at a minimum. Grouping them together helps keep them balanced, which will improve Ross's presentation.

Option 2: This is an incorrect choice. Ross should have a balance across the types of content he uses. Using a lot of case studies but very few facts can imbalance the presentation and give it less variety.

Option 3: This is a correct choice. By including intense moments, Ross gets the audience excited. By including relaxed periods, he lets them settle down and reflect. This variation in his style will keep the audience engaged.

Option 4: This is a correct choice. Questions and statements are both important types of content to provide. The statements provide content Ross wants to deliver. Questions will open his presentation to his audience participation.

Option 5: This is an incorrect choice. A presentation of mostly facts will make Ross's presentation boring. He should balance them with case studies, statements and questions. That will give his presentation nice content variety.

Option 6: This is a correct choice. Not all case studies should be the same length. Some may need to be long, while others can be quite brief. Using one to illustrate each part is a good way for Ross to maintain variety.

Bob makes sales presentations several times a week. He comes across as a pretty laid-back guy--that's part of his persuasive charm. But he makes sure that he does not rely on this alone to make a sale. His delivery style is characterized by plenty of variety.

Low intensity

"When I want the client to think hard about the benefits of an offer, I stand or sit still, without saying anything. That can be a helpful, low-intensity moment."

High intensity

"I like to lay the basic facts of the product before the client very fast and energetically. For me, that's a high-intensity time."

There is more than one way to achieve a high-energy period in your presentation. You can talk faster, like Bob, or a little louder. If you do either or both of these things, you will become more animated, and the overall impression will be of increased intensity. The reverse is also true, so silence and stillness equals low intensity. It is an excellent way to invite the audience to think, as Bob does.

For most of your presentation, you will use your normal, conversational level of intensity. But remember, a successful presentation contains periods of high and low intensity in each section.

As with delivery techniques, there should be a variety of content in each main part of your presentation. The different kinds of content support each other and make the presentation stronger.

facts

Use facts to provide the overview of a story. For example: "These are the key facts." Also use groups of facts to focus on detail: "Let me explain exactly how this part of the machine is assembled." But remember, if you provide all the detail, the audience will lose the general picture.

statements and questions

A statement, perhaps in the form of a single sentence, is often used to introduce a new section in the presentation or a significant new part within a section. Questions can be rhetorical, like, "Is this a good idea?" They can invite reflection: "What should we do?"

case studies

Use a case study to illustrate a statement or for fleshing out facts. You can introduce it by saying, "Let me give you an example of what I mean" or "This is how it worked in practice."

Colleen has given thought to her delivery. It's clear that her introductory statement will be a moment of low-intensity delivery. In contrast, she will move through the detailed figures rapidly to avoid boredom. The case study, "Love Me For Ever," requires high intensity to illustrate her emotional commitment.

The presentation contains statements and a question, groups of facts, and one important case study. She should also use case studies, short or long, in the other parts of her presentation.

There is a severe lack of variety in the first 20 minutes of William's presentation. The first thing he must address is the way he uses facts. He should be more selective and make a clear separation in his own mind between overview facts used to provide the story and facts used to focus on detail.

William delivers all of his presentation at a steady pace, which isn't good. He needs peaks of high and low intensity. He also needs questions and statements to signal important moments. Monotony is not interesting. Maintain the interest of the people in your audience by offering them variety. But remember, the variety should also be relevant.

TECHNIQUES THAT ALLOW A SPEAKER TO RELATE TO THE AUDIENCE

Techniques that allow a speaker to relate to the audience

Most people are outgoing. Generally speaking, when they come into contact with other people, they want to form some kind of relationship, and this is as true in a presentation situation as in any other form of interaction.

One of the "wow factors" that makes a presentation special is the speaker, simply through the language that he or she uses, encouraging and developing a relationship with the audience.

An audience wants a relationship with a speaker; but what kind of relationship is appropriate?

Isaac was at a conference recently where the speaker established exactly the right kind of relationship and avoided an inappropriate relationship.

appropriate

"She said things that allowed me to get to know her personally. She also said things that showed she was interested in me and the other people in the audience."

inappropriate

"She did not give sensitive information about herself. She also avoided any inquiries into my private life."

The techniques you need to establish personal interaction are the same for all audiences, although you may need to work a little harder with a large audience.

Question

Your colleague, Gary, wants to know how he should interact with his presentation audiences. What do you say?

Options:

1. "Tell them sensitive, personal information about yourself."

2. "Tell your audience things that allow the audience members to get to know you personally."

3. "Say things to your audience that show an interest in the audience members."

4. "Ask about the personal lives of the audience members."

Answer:

You should say things to the audience that allow people to get to know you. You also need to say things that show an interest in your audience.

Option 1: This is an incorrect choice. While Gary wants to build a relationship with his audience, sharing sensitive personal information is not a good way to do that. Gary can share non-sensitive personal information.

Option 2: This is a correct choice. Gary can share non-sensitive personal information with his audience. That will help them feel like they know Gary without it being uncomfortable. This way, Gary builds a good relationship with his audience.

Option 3: This choice is correct. The audience likes to know that the presenter is interested in them. If Gary demonstrates his care for their interests, the audience will warm up to him and interact with him.

Option 4: This is an incorrect choice. The audience members do not want a close personal relationship. Gary is trying to build an appropriate business relationship. Personal information is inappropriate.

Enrico, the new regional manager at Phoebus Holidays, has paid a surprise visit to the main reservations center to give everyone a pep talk. It's the first time they've met him and, frankly, Paola and Louis are not at all impressed.

Paola: This guy is very polite, but he seems so remote. I don't feel I know where he's coming from.

Louis: His tone's enthusiastic enough, but I'd like to know what he really thinks.

Paola: He certainly doesn't seem to know anything about the special conditions in this facility. He could be giving this talk anywhere in any facility, and he'd be doing it in precisely the same way.

Enrico may be able to repair the damage later, but his presentation is a frustrating experience for the audience members because they want interaction and there is none. So what should Enrico have done? What is the correct way to relate to an audience in order to build a relationship?

allow your audience to get to know you

Let your audience get to know you by revealing information about yourself in the book of the presentation and by revealing your own personal views or feelings from time to time.

show an interest in your audience

Instead of ignoring the audience, which is what Enrico did, you should use facts that show a specific knowledge of the audience members and also refer to their feelings or state of mind.

Audiences and circumstances differ widely, of book, and you have to adapt the information you reveal about yourself and the level of interest you show in your audience to suit the context.

However, the basic requirement does not change: You must encourage the natural interaction that the audience wants.

Question

Your colleagues have just come back from the New Options conference, and they are talking about how each of the five presenters behaved. Which statements indicate the presenter was interactive in the way he or she talked to the audience?

Options:

1. "From time to time, he introduced some information that showed a particular knowledge of the audience."

2. "This guy certainly told us a number of things about himself and let us know what his own views were."

3. "Most of the time he was a clear and professional communicator."

4. "At some points, he talked about what we were thinking and feeling."

5. "She made a number of polite and very respectful remarks."

Answer:

Giving Successful Presentations

Showing interactivity involves revealing information about yourself and your views, using facts about the audience, and making reference to the feelings or state of mind of the audience.

Option 1: This is a correct choice. Audiences and settings vary widely. They like to know that a presenter is there for just them. If your colleagues include such information, their audiences will be more open to interaction.

Option 2: This is a correct choice. One way for a speaker to be interactive is to share a few things about himself and to share his views from time to time. That way, an audience feels like they get to know the speaker.

Option 3: This is an incorrect choice. While communicating clearly and professionally is important for a good presentation, it does not foster interaction. A speaker should show knowledge of the audience and say a few things about himself.

Option 4: This choice is correct. A good way to interact with the audience is to demonstrate knowledge of them. When a speaker makes statements that shows he knows what the audience is thinking, they will interact with him more.

Option 5: This is an incorrect choice. She could have made those remarks to any audience. An audience wants to hear some statements geared specifically for them. This shows interest in them instead of ignoring them.

If you know your audience well already, interaction is usually easier. If you have not already met the people you will be speaking to, you need to find out more about them at the preparation stage.

A month after his first presentation, Enrico visits Phoebus Holidays' reservations center again to talk to everyone about the new call-handling procedure. This time he's better informed about his audience, so he does a much better job of forming a relationship with people.

Paola, along with everyone else, really likes the way he shows an interest in them.

Know the audience

"He said, 'I know which parts of the procedure are causing difficulty, and I'll go through them.' He also said, 'I understand from your supervisor, Judith, that you've undergone a lot of changes recently.' He was really on top of the facts."

Refer to feelings

"He said, 'I hear some of you don't like the procedure, but I've also been told that there's a great team spirit in the center, so I'm confident you'll make it work.' He showed that he knew what we were feeling, and he also empathized with us."

Enrico's audience members warmed to the fact that he knew about their concerns and was responding to them.

The other thing that helped Enrico to form a bond with his audience was that this time, he did not settle for being polite but distant. Instead, he projected himself as a unique human being.

Louis responded strongly to this.

reveal personal information

"He said, 'I worked in a center just like this until a couple of years ago' and told us a little about that. And he said, 'I've just moved into the area last week, so I'll be around more often now. You may even see me at the hockey games.'"

express personal opinions

"He said, 'My own view about the new procedure is that it's not perfect yet, but it's a big improvement.' And he told us he regretted not visiting for a whole month, but he was determined it wouldn't happen again. I got to know what he was thinking and feeling."

To really impress audience members, you have to break down barriers. At the same time, you clearly cannot reveal things about yourself of a personal nature that might embarrass them or cause offense. If in doubt, err on the side of caution.

It is good to show an interest in a client by using forms of words that attribute thoughts or feelings. Expressions like "I'm sure you're wondering..." or "I know you're concerned about..." or "I know you'll want to hear about..." work well.

Case Study: Question 1 of 2
Scenario

You have been transferred to a different office at Lux Bathrooms to take over the order processing function. You have introduced yourself and had a few words with each individual team member during the morning. Now, after lunch, you are about to explain new procedures and paperwork to the office staff.

Answer the questions, in order, to show how you will relate to your audience.

Question

You have just started your presentation, and you are giving some background. You want your audience to build a relationship with you by getting to know you. What do you say?

Options:

1. "The new procedures have already been successfully tried elsewhere."
2. "My previous boss, Lisa, who's really innovative, developed this system, and I found it saved a lot of time."
3. "I don't like a lot of paperwork, so I'm always looking for ways to reduce it."
4. "I've always wanted to be promoted to a job like this. I'm just concerned that my family won't be supportive."
5. "The policy of Lux Bathrooms is that paperwork and procedures should always be kept to a minimum."

Answer:

You should encourage the audience to build a relationship with you by revealing information about your previous boss and your feelings about paperwork. You should not reveal sensitive personal information.

Option 1: This is an incorrect choice. This statement does not reveal any information about you to the Lux Bathroom audience. You may want to share your work background or other information so that the audience can connect with you.

Option 2: This is a correct choice. By giving some information about your boss being the developer, you are sharing personal information the audience can relate to. You've also expressed your opinion, which makes you more real to the audience.

Option 3: This choice is correct. This statement reveals an appropriate bit of information about yourself. It also is a statement of opinion that will help you sell the changes and build relationships better.

Option 4: This is an incorrect choice. Any personal information you share should be appropriate. This type of information is too sensitive and will be uncomfortable for your audience. Keep the relationship professional.

Option 5: This choice is incorrect. This statement reveals nothing about you personally and seems cold and distant. Try sharing a little something about yourself that your audience members can relate to.

Case Study: Question 2 of 2

You are now into your description of the detail of the new procedure and paperwork, supported by a slide showing one of the new forms. You want to show that you are interested in the audience. What do you say?

Options:

1. "I don't know what you think about the old form, but this is the new one."

2. "I was talking to Anna and Jim this morning, and I know that the version of the form you've been using is a lot different from this one."

3. "This is an example of one of the new forms. Take a look at it."

4. "From what I've been told, nobody's exactly in love with the old form."

5. "I'm sure you're wondering how long this form will take to complete."

Answer:

You build your relationship with the audience by revealing a knowledge of their feelings and by knowing things about them (in this case, about their old form). You also attribute thoughts to them.

Option 1: This is an incorrect choice. You want to demonstrate that you know what your audience is thinking or feeling. You should also show that you care. A statement about how they feel about the form, followed by your opinion, would be better.

Option 2: This is a correct choice. By saying this, it reveals that you know your specific audience and have taken the time to find out what their concerns are. This engages them more and helps them feel like you are speaking only to them.

Option 3: This is an incorrect choice. This comment does not connect with the specific audience in any way. A better statement would be one that reveals you understand how the audience feels about the old and new forms.

Option 4: This is a correct choice. You want to demonstrate that you know what they're thinking and how they feel and that you care about your audience. This statement reveals that you've done your homework and know the audience.

Option 5: This is a correct choice. This statement shows that you know what your audience is thinking. It makes your presentation feel more personalized and interactive, which the audience will appreciate.

It was a good idea to talk about your old boss. You revealed something about yourself, but it was relevant and not particularly personal. As you get to know your team, you will probably divulge more personal information, but personal information always has to be appropriate to the occasion.

You took the opportunity to find out about the old procedures and how your team felt about them by talking with people in the morning. You were then able to use this information to build your relationship with them in your presentation.

Giving Successful Presentations

Making a great presentation involves more than communicating in a dynamic and interesting way. You are in a room with other human beings. Make your presentation memorable by relating to them on a human level.

TECHNIQUES OF FILMMAKERS USED IN PRESENTATIONS

Techniques of filmmakers used in presentations

Make a list of the top five movies you've seen. What makes them so great? Are there any lessons you can learn from them and apply to make your presentations memorable?

If you're watching a movie on television and you're not enjoying it, you change channels or turn it off. If you go to a movie theater and the film bores you, you take your revenge by warning your friends not to go.

Moviemakers know you have these choices, so they work hard to make their movies gripping from start to finish. Follow along as Kristina and Frank are discussing the movies they saw on television last night.

Kristina: I watched a science fiction movie. I like science fiction, and it was gripping to begin with, but then after a while it was impossible to follow the story. I simply lost interest.

Giving Successful Presentations

Frank: I watched a comedy. A few scenes made me laugh, and the music was great, but the characters were dull. I'd seen them all before in other movies.

It is not enough to like the subject of a movie or find it interesting in the beginning or enjoyable in parts. To be memorable, it has to:

- capture your attention at the start,
- hold your attention throughout.

Question

Evelyn is pretty sure that she can improve her presentations by using the same techniques as moviemakers, but she is not sure what to aim for. She asks you for advice. What do you tell her?

Options:

1. "Like a movie, your presentation has to be interesting in parts."

2. "Your presentation must capture audience attention at the beginning, just like a movie."

3. "Just like a memorable movie, your presentation needs to be about a subject the audience is already interested in."

4. "Memorable movies hold the audience until the end, and your presentations have to do the same."

Answer

The lesson that presentations should take from movies is the need to capture the audience at the start and hold them until the end.

Option 1: This is an incorrect choice. A good presentation should be interesting throughout. Evelyn should capture the audience from the very beginning and keep them engaged all along.

Option 2: This is a correct choice. Evelyn needs to make sure her audience is paying attention from the start. Good movies get people engaged immediately and stay interesting all along. Evelyn's presentations should do the same.

Option 3: This is an incorrect choice. The audience may or may not already have an interest in her topic. However, Evelyn should capture their interest at the very beginning and hold their attention throughout the entire presentation.

Option 4: This choice is correct. Evelyn's presentations should keep her audiences engaged the entire time. Otherwise, they may get bored in the middle and lose interest. A good presentation doesn't lag in parts.

So how exactly does a great movie manage to keep you on the edge of your seat? What are the techniques involved that are transferable to your presentations?

Spence has directed many movies, and he knows that all highly successful movies do two things really well: They tell stories, and they create characters. It is these qualities in a movie that engage the people in an audience and make them respond.

tell stories

"Every movie tells a story, and the stories that work best are simple ones. The story also needs drama and excitement to keep the audience fully involved."

create characters

"Great movie characters come alive. They have strong personalities. Also, the audience has to be able to identify with them."

Of book, most movies aim to entertain, and they employ complicated technical wizardry and professional actors to do it. Your resources are more limited, and the primary objective of your presentation is not usually entertainment. Nevertheless, when you make a presentation, you are a storyteller.

If you want your presentation to fully engage your audience members, you must create strong characters and tell a story that is easy to follow.

When Regina was promoted to manager, she was expected to give presentations. She found that at the beginning of her presentations, her audience members were usually fidgety or looked bored. She transformed the situation for the better by recognizing that a presentation was a kind of story, and that like any other storyteller, she had to follow the basic rules.

keep the story simple

"I link a small number of connected points, relevant to the audience, only including necessary detail. I use language to organize the story. For example, I'll say: 'The situation we have now started last December when...' or 'We are going to do three things in the following order...'"

inject excitement

"I create a sense of anticipation. For example, I'll say: 'What are we going to do about this? I'll tell you in a moment.' I make sure my presentation has several peaks, or periods when the action I'm describing is particularly intense and interesting."

Question

When your team members make presentations, the audience is often turned off for a good deal of time. You decide to help your team members by pointing out how they can transfer the skills of moviemakers to public speaking situations in order to keep the audience engaged. What do you say?

Options:

1. "Your story should have characters with strong personalities."

2. "Your presentation must tell a story using sophisticated electronic effects."

3. "Your presentation must tell a simple story for your audience."

4. "In order to make the characters in your story come alive, you need trained acting skills."

5. "You must inject dramatic, exciting moments into your presentation to maintain audience interest."

6. "The audience needs to be able to identify with the characters in your story."

Answer:

Your presentation, like a good movie, requires a simple story with moments of excitement and drama. It should also have characters with strong personalities that are easy to identify with.

Option 1: This is a correct choice. Strong characters come alive for the audience. They make the presentation memorable, and audience members can identify with the characters. This keeps them engaged with the story you're telling them.

Option 2: This is an incorrect choice. While you may want to use electronic effects, they are not necessary for a good story. A good story has a simple plot line and strong characters. These will keep your audience engaged.

Option 3: This is a correct choice. Simple stories work far better than complex ones, as they are easier to follow.

Giving Successful Presentations

A good story also has drama and excitement to keep the audience involved.

Option 4: This choice is incorrect. Great characters have strong personalities, and audiences can identify with them. You don't have to have good acting skills to give these qualities to the characters in your story.

Option 5: This choice is correct. All good stories need drama and excitement. These keep the audience engaged, wondering what will happen next. Your presentation should include some drama and excitement in its story.

Option 6: This is a correct choice. If the audience identifies with the characters, they will stay interested in the story you are telling. This also makes it easier for them to follow the story since they can relate to it.

Follow along as Regina critiques the presentation she gave this morning to the telephone sales team.

There were just a few major points to the story, and they were connected naturally for the audience: Last month they followed the script, and they did a great job converting leads into sales; this month some of them did their own thing and they were way short of the goal; next month they've got to go back to the script.

It was a good idea to tell the sales team early on that I was going to play back some of the calls we'd monitored-- that really built up a sense of anticipation.

And playing the calls back to the sales team during the presentation provided dramatic peaks. The team members were really interested to hear how the calls that departed from the script failed to make a sale and how those that followed the script were successful.

In the past, I would have included a lot of data about calls in the presentation and probably gone through parts of the script word by word, but all that detail would have turned off the sales team.

Regina knows that her audience will only remain in the grip of her story if the characters in it are interesting. How does she inject her presentations with strong, lively characters?

Create strong personalities

"People need to be able to visualize the characters. I'll say: 'This CEO was a distinguished-looking guy in his fifties with a great sense of humor' and give an example of something he said. I'll also describe a place, a factory, or a special object."

Invoke identification

"The audience needs to know what people in your story are thinking and feeling in order to identify with them. I'll say: 'They were impressed' or 'They were a little down.' I'll describe the atmosphere of places: 'It's a really energetic office,' for example."

In a presentation, you, the speaker, are the strongest character. It is your animation and energy that will make your story and the characters in it come alive for the audience.

Give them strong personalities

"I'm going to describe Heidi, the really energetic woman who tested Gone, our bathroom cleanser. At the end of the trial, she kept saying: 'Give me more of this.' I'll also describe the bathrooms she cleaned--they had the dirtiest white tiles you ever saw before she went to work on them."

Allow audience to identify with them

"I'll tell the audience how Heidi, who had her own cleaning business, really liked Thorough's products. A lot of cleaning products left her feeling frustrated, but not ours. She was a great woman--I could feel her energy in the office whenever I visited her."

Heidi obviously has a powerful personality, and Stuart's description allows us to visualize her and the way she transforms bathrooms with the aid of Thorough Inc.'s product. We learn about her feelings and also the atmosphere she creates at work.

Heidi is a sympathetic character, and it is easy to identify with her. She will help Stuart to hold the audience's total attention.

Case Study: Question 1 of 2
Scenario

Amanda Toby, the granddaughter of the founder of Toby's Outdoor Furniture, has rented space at the House and Gardens Exhibition. As a way of generating more interest, she will give a presentation about Toby's products from her booth three times a day at set times.

Answer the questions to show how much Amanda uses the techniques of moviemakers to hold her audience.

Question

Amanda is concerned about making her presentation gripping throughout--like a good movie. How will her techniques help her to do this?

Options:

1. Amanda's presentation tells a simple story.
2. Her presentation is exciting.
3. Her presentation has characters with strong personalities.
4. She creates characters people can identify with.

Answer:

Amanda's notes indicate she is planning to use all the techniques needed for a gripping presentation, except one: She doesn't include characters with strong personalities.

Option 1: This is a correct choice. Amanda is going to limit her story to a few historical facts about their company and furniture. This will help her stress the main point of the story without losing it in too much detail.

Option 2: This is a correct choice. Amanda plans to get people excited about actually sitting in their chairs. She will do that by having chairs there for them and stressing their comfort. That way, the audience will act upon Amanda's words.

Option 3: This is an incorrect choice. Amanda is not planning on telling any specific stories about customers. She plans to tell them general responses from people, but nothing specific that creates a strong character or impression.

Option 4: This is a correct choice. By telling them they'll understand why others like their chairs when they sit on them, Amanda is helping the audience identify with others' stories about the chairs.

Case Study: Question 2 of 2

What could Amanda do to make her presentation more enthralling for her audience?

Options:

1. Amanda could give the audience a lot more information about the origins of the company.
2. She should make her grandfather come alive as a strong character by describing how he labored alongside his

   workers to achieve Toby quality.

Giving Successful Presentations

3. Amanda should inject as much excitement into the presentation as possible to keep the audience entertained.

4. Amanda could describe one particular garden with Toby furniture in it and how relaxing the atmosphere is.

5. She should explicitly describe the construction methods used on Toby furniture.

Answer:

Amanda should describe her grandfather and the atmosphere in one garden, which will create characters with strong personalities. She should not add a lot of unnecessary detail or turn her presentation into a piece of entertainment.

Option 1: This is an incorrect choice. Amanda is doing a good job by keeping the story simple. It is simple because she is including so few details. Amanda could make her grandfather feel real or tell a specific story about the furniture.

Option 2: This choice is correct. Amanda could create a strong feel for the character of her grandfather. That will make people feel like they know the company better, which will make them feel better about her presentation.

Option 3: Incorrect. Amanda's job is to present on the company and the furniture, not entertain the audience. She has enough excitement built in. She should probably tell a story about her grandfather or the furniture to make it come alive.

Option 4: This is a correct choice. By telling a specific story about the furniture, Amanda is giving the audience something they can identify with. The relaxing atmosphere sounds inviting, and the audience will want that same thing.

Option 5: This choice is incorrect. Describing the construction methods may be too much impersonal detail. Instead, Amanda should tell a few stories or choose a good character to bring to life that her audience can relate to.

Amanda's opening remark, stating that she will talk about what makes Toby's furniture great, creates some excitement for the audience right away. When she says she's going to invite people to try the furniture, she's doing the same thing. Her story is extremely simple, and the audience will be able to follow it easily; it's all connected to the fact that Toby furniture is great.

Amanda tells the audience what people feel about Toby furniture, which gives them characters to identify with. The only real weakness is a lack of characters with strong personalities; she includes neither people nor places.

Your presentation is not trying to compete with a movie, but you need to know how to apply the basic techniques that enable the professionals to hold an audience by telling a story and creating characters.

CHAPTER 3 - AVAILABLE PRESENTATION RESOURCES

CHAPTER 3 - Available Presentation Resources
   SECTION 1 - Making the Most of Visual Aids
   SECTION 2 - Dealing with Questions during Your Presentation
   SECTION 3 - Effective Team Presentations

SECTION 1 - MAKING THE MOST OF VISUAL AIDS

SECTION 1 - Making the Most of Visual Aids

Slides projected onto a screen, flip charts, white boards, and handouts are the most common types of visual aids used in business presentations. If used correctly, they provide support for the speaker and the audience at the same time.

Many presenters abuse visual aids. This topic shows you how you can make effective use of visuals and enhance the quality of your presentations.

The computer adds a wonderful, new dimension to the presenter's art. You can produce your own slides, achieving professional-quality animations, artwork, and sound. However, the power of presentation software should be used with caution.

MAKING APPROPRIATE USE OF QUESTIONS

Making appropriate use of questions

Many presenters believe that their job is to talk, and the audience's job is to listen. Questions from the audience? No, thank you. Does this describe you? The members of your audience are interested in what you're saying, so they want a chance to ask you questions about your presentation.

Mai and George have just attended a presentation. What did they think about it?

Mai: That was a great presentation. He was a really interesting guy.

George: I wish I could have asked him questions about some of the technical stuff.

I didn't understand all of it.

Mai: It was a bit controversial at times. There were a couple of things I would have liked the opportunity to challenge him on.

George: Unfortunately, questions weren't on his agenda. We couldn't ask any questions, and he didn't ask us any questions either.

The speaker stimulated Mai and George's interest, but by not taking questions, he frustrated them at the same time. The fact that he did not ask questions added to their sense of detachment from the speaker.

Natalie is a marketing consultant who talks to several audiences every week. She would never dream of making a presentation without including questions. She knows that asking and receiving questions, although not a panacea, pays off in significant ways.

Comment 1

"Questions make me responsive to the audience by allowing me to find out what people are thinking. They also help me to have a collaborative relationship."

Comment 2

"Promoting questions is no guarantee that the audience will agree with me or like me."

Question

You often meet with other speakers who are reluctant to ask questions during their presentations or take questions from audience members, but you are convinced of the benefits of questions. What do you say to the other speakers to convince them of the value?

Options:

1. "Questions make a speaker react more responsively to the audience."

2. "They ensure that the audience agrees with what the speaker is saying."

3. "Questions make the audience members like the speaker."

Giving Successful Presentations

4. "They encourage a relationship in which the audience and the speaker are collaborating."

Answer:

In fact, questions make the speaker more responsive to the audience, as well as promoting a collaborative relationship.

Option 1: This choice is correct. Without taking questions, a speaker cannot know what the audience is interested in knowing more about. Questions allow the speaker to respond to their interests and curiosities.

Option 2: This is an incorrect choice. Questions do not guarantee that the audience will agree with you. However, the audience will feel more comfortable and less frustrated with a speaker who allows and answers questions.

Option 3: This choice is incorrect. Although a speaker may invite questions, it is not a guarantee the audience will like him. The audience will, however, feel more comfortable and be less frustrated with the speaker.

Option 4: This is a correct choice. By taking questions, the speaker is allowing the audience to interact with him or her. This makes the audience feel like the speaker is more approachable and interested in what they have to say or want to know.

Audiences expect you to ask and take questions, and you must be ready to meet this expectation.

HANDLING THE QUESTION-AND-ANSWER PHASE

Handling the question-and-answer phase
A speaker will usually set aside a period of time at the end of her presentation for the audience to ask questions.

A question-and-answer session at the end of your speech provides a great opportunity for interaction, but how do you ensure that it is successful?

Mike is nearing the end of his presentation.

Well, ladies and gentlemen, I thought there might be time to take a few questions from you.

Unfortunately, I can see that we're out of time. Sorry about that, folks.

Mike is typical of a lot of presenters. He knows that a question-and-answer session is a good idea but, probably because he fears he may not be able to answer all the questions, he finds an excuse to avoid it.

For successful question-and-answer sessions, it is not necessary to answer all the questions from the audience. However, it is necessary that you:

- really want to have a question-and-answer session,

Giving Successful Presentations

- are proactive about the question-and-answer session during your presentation.

Question

You decide to write a list to remind yourself of the basic requirements of a successful question-and-answer session. What do you include on your list?

Options:

1. The speaker must be proactive about the question-and-answer phase during the presentation.

2. The speaker will be able to answer all the questions from the audience.

3. The speaker has to want a question-and-answer session.

4. The speaker will make the session as short as possible.

Answer:

A speaker must want a question-and-answer session, and make this clear to his audience.

Option 1: This choice is correct. As the speaker, you must be the one to make sure a question-and-answer session happens. Your audience cannot force one on you. You should ensure you leave enough time for their questions.

Option 2: Incorrect choice. You probably will not be able to answer every question. However, the audience is more concerned that you appear willing to try to answer their questions. Be proactive about including a question-and-answer session.

Option 3: This is a correct choice. As the speaker, you have to want a question-and-answer session and be proactive about it for one to happen. If you do not want a session, it will not happen. This will be very frustrating for your audience.

Option 4: This is an incorrect choice. Leave plenty of time for a question-and-answer session. That way, you are sure to get in enough questions so the audience does not feel frustrated. If the session is too short, they will feel shortchanged.

Concluding with a question session is extremely common and very useful. This topic focuses on a strategy for running a dynamic question session at the end of your talk. This does not mean that you should not take questions at any other time. A few questions during your presentation are a sign of audience interest. However, if you answer a lot of questions during your presentation, it is likely to be extremely disruptive.

A safe strategy, particularly for the less experienced speaker, is to encourage questions at the end of your presentation, rather than during it. Announce at the beginning that you intend to have a question-and-answer session at the end.

Paola's presentations are lively and usually end with lots of questions from the audience. Verne thinks audience questions are a great idea, but he doesn't know how to encourage them. He asks Paola what her secret is.

Verne: What do I need to do?

Paola: First of all, you need to anticipate questions.

Verne: You mean think about the questions before I stand up to speak?

Paola: Exactly. And you need to tell the audience how you want to handle questions. If you are going to finish with a question-and-answer session, you must announce it at the start of your presentation. And finally, you must allow time for questions.

Verne: That sounds simple enough.

If you truly want to answer questions from your audience, then you will think about them at the planning stage. You will not wait to think about them until you are standing in front of your audience.

Also, you will be proactive during your presentation. As Paola says, you have to announce your policy on questions to the audience. Tell people you are going to have a question session and that you are looking forward to it.

Question

You are determined to have a great question-and-answer session in your next presentation. What will you do to make this happen?

Options:

1. make sure that I allow sufficient time for questions
2. think about questions while I am planning my presentation
3. encourage questions by standing close to my audience
4. tell my audience that I have set aside a period for questions at the end of my presentation
5. not think about questions at the planning stage

Answer:

For a question-and-answer session to be successful, you have to plan for questions, allow sufficient time for questions, and tell your audience how you are going to handle them.

Option 1: This choice is correct. The audience should have plenty of time to ask their questions. Announce at the beginning of the presentation when that time will be, and do not let your presentation spill over.

Option 2: Correct choice. The time to think about questions is before your presentation, not during it. Anticipate what people might ask so you feel better prepared. You may have to research your audience to anticipate their questions.

Option 3: This is an incorrect choice. The audience may not interpret that signal correctly. Instead, invite questions by announcing the start of a question-and-answer session. That will cue the audience to begin asking their questions.

Option 4: This choice is correct. Let your audience know that you will allow time for them to ask questions at the end. That way, they'll hold most of their questions during your presentation. However, ensure you give them that time.

Option 5: This is an incorrect choice. To the contrary, consider possible questions during the planning stage. By doing so, you can plan for what the audience might ask you and prepare good responses in advance.

Making presentations is a major part of Paola's job as office manager at GD Recruitment. The lively question sessions that follow her talks are the result of the fact that she not only understands the basics of encouraging a good question-and-answer session, but she also knows how to put those basics into practice.

Plan

"When I'm planning a talk, I list the specific questions that I expect the audience to ask on the topic, and I prepare answers. It helps me if I know my audience well.

Giving Successful Presentations

If not, I have to research the audience in order to anticipate questions."

Announce

"In my introduction, I announce that I'll have a question session at the end of my talk. I encourage questions by using positive language, so I'll say something like: 'I have allowed plenty of time for questions at the end.'"

Allow time

"I allow time for questions, and I do not permit my presentation to encroach on that time. I announce the question session, and then I pause and wait. Sometimes I suggest a question. I'll say, 'You may still be wondering about....'"

In your introductory remarks, ask the people in your audience to make a mental note during your presentation of questions they would like to ask. This will promote an energetic question-and-answer session.

Sometimes, audience members are hesitant at the start of a question session. Suggesting a question that the audience may want to ask is a way of breaking an initial silence at the end of your talk.

Someone in your audience may well surprise you with a question that you cannot answer. This is not a problem. Simply say that you will get back to him or her with an answer later.

Mike's boss usually introduces new employees at Plasta Packaging to the work of the repair and maintenance department, but yesterday, Mike stood in for him for the first time. Mike talked for half an hour, which included time for questions. After his presentation, Mike talked to his boss about it.

Presentation planning

"I'm glad I asked you what questions these new employees usually ask. It was a big help to know they ask questions about the causes of particular breakdowns; as a result, I'd rehearsed a couple examples of breakdowns to use in the question session."

Presentation: Introductory remarks

"At the beginning, I said, 'I'm going to talk for 20 minutes and allow ten minutes for questions. As I'm talking, make a mental note of all the questions you want to ask. I promise I'll do my best to deal with them.'"

Presentation: Q & A Session

"After 20 minutes, I said, 'That's it. Now it's your turn. I'm sure you're eager to ask lots of questions, and I want to answer them.' Then I waited. It took half a minute or so, but the questions started to come."

Mike did all the right things to encourage an animated question-and-answer session. The type of audience was new to him, but asking his boss's advice allowed him to anticipate questions realistically.

He made it clear from the beginning that he welcomed questions and there would be time for questions at the end of his presentation. At the same time, he encouraged the new employees to think of questions as he was talking.

Mike announced the start of the question session in a positive way and was not afraid to wait. He gave the people in his audience a little time to gather their thoughts and the courage to start asking questions.

Case Study: Question 1 of 2
Scenario

Virginia works for Keen Investments. She was recently promoted to an investment executive, and she now has

Giving Successful Presentations

her own portfolio of corporate clients. After she gave her first client presentation--to Evans Corporation, explaining her investment strategy for it--Virginia's boss asked her to write a short report reviewing her approach to the presentation.

Select the learning aid Virginias' Report for information on her approach to the question-and-answer phase of her presentation, and then answer the questions that follow, in order.

Question

How effective was Virginia's approach to the question-and-answer phase of her presentation?

Options:

1. At the planning stage, Virginia shows that she wants the Evans management team to ask questions.

2. At the start of her presentation, she is proactive in relation to questions.

3. At the end of her talk, she is proactive in relation to questions.

Answer:

In fact, Virginia showed at the planning stage that she wanted a question-and-answer session and was proactive in her approach to questions at the end of her presentation, but not at the beginning.

Option 1: This is a correct choice. Virginia anticipated and researched possible questions and answers early. She spoke with her predecessor about what to expect and was prepared for the questions her audience asked.

Option 2: This choice is incorrect. Virginia did indicate the length of her talk but was not proactive about questions at that point. She waited until the start of the question-and-answer session to announce that she was willing to take questions.

Option 3: This choice is correct. Virginia announced that she would be taking questions when she got to the end of her presentation. She left plenty of time to take questions and answer them thoroughly.

Case Study: Question 2 of 2

How could Virginia have improved her approach to the question-and-answer phase of her presentation?

Options:

1. As part of her introductory remarks, Virginia could have said something like, "First, I want to explain my proposed strategy. Then I look forward to answering all of your questions."

2. She should have allowed a question-and-answer session but reduced the amount of time allocated to it.

3. At the start of her presentation, Virginia should have indicated how she intended to handle questions.

4. At the start of her presentation, she could have suggested that people should make a mental note of questions as she was speaking.

5. Virginia should have put her question-and-answer session at the beginning of her presentation, rather than the end.

Answer:

In fact, at the start of her presentation, Virginia should have indicated that there would be a question session after her presentation, and she should have invited the audience members to make a mental note of questions.

Option 1: This is a correct choice. Virginia did not let her audience know at the beginning that she would be taking questions. She could have announced to the audience that time would be left for questions at the end.

Option 2: This is an incorrect choice. Virginia did exactly what she planned and stuck with the presentation length she announced to the audience. This helped the audience set expectations and plan the questions they wanted to ask.

Option 3: This choice is correct. Virginia announced how long her talk would be but did not let the audience know how questions would be handled. Informing audiences at the beginning of the presentation helps them know what to expect.

Option 4: This choice is correct. She could have facilitated this point better. If audience members noted their questions as she talked, the question session would be more energetic, since they would have notes of what they want to ask.

Option 5: This is an incorrect choice. After the presentation is the best time for the question-and-answer session. However, letting the audience know how she was planning to handle their questions would help them know what to expect.

Virginia did a good job in most respects. Because she was not familiar with the people in her audience, she could not anticipate their questions on the strategy. So she used her colleague as a source of information about questions.

She made it clear at the end of her talk that she expected and wanted questions and had allowed time for questions. When she was asked a question that she could not answer, she dealt with it in a businesslike way.

However, Virginia's approach had two major weaknesses. She should have announced at the start of her presentation that she had allowed time for a question session. She also should have suggested that the managers make mental notes of questions that came to mind as she was speaking.

Don't leave the success of your question-and-answer sessions to chance. Plan for success, and be proactive during your talk.

QUESTIONS THAT ELICIT A DESIRED RESPONSE

Questions that elicit a desired response
Think about the best presenters you've ever seen. It is almost certain that all of them involved their audience members by asking them questions. Anna is an experienced presenter. She asks a lot of questions during her extremely productive presentations.

direct
"I ask questions to the whole audience and to individuals in the audience-- questions demanding a substantial response."

rhetorical
"I also ask rhetorical questions. I'll say, 'Now, what can we do about this situation?' And then I'll give the audience the answer."

A rhetorical question is a device used by a speaker to command attention; it does not need a direct response. A speaker also often asks questions to check audience understanding; she'll say, "Is that clear?" or "OK?" This type of question only calls for a limited audience response.

On the other hand, questions that demand a direct and substantial audience response stimulate significant audience involvement in the presentation.

Question

Matt wants to know what kind of questions he should ask during his presentations to encourage significant audience involvement. What do you say to him?

Options:

1. "Ask questions to check that the people in your audience understand what you have said to them."

2. "Ask rhetorical questions of the audience."

3. "Ask questions that require audience members to do later research."

4. "Ask questions that require a direct and substantial response from the audience."

Answer:

In fact, questions that require the audience members to react directly and to a substantial extent will produce significant audience involvement.

Option 1: This choice is incorrect. This type of question involves a very minimal response from the audience and will not elicit much audience involvement. Instead, Matt should ask genuine, open questions that require a substantial response.

Option 2: Incorrect choice. Rhetorical questions are ones Matt doesn't expect the audience to actually answer and will not encourage much involvement. To encourage audience involvement, he should ask questions that require a response.

Option 3: This choice is incorrect. If Matt wants audience involvement, he wants them to participate during the presentation, not later. Instead of asking them to do something later, he should ask questions that require an immediate response.

Option 4: This is the correct choice. If Matt wants the audience to interact with him, he will need to ask questions that require responses. Such questions require the audience to think about their responses and formulate an answer.

When Bob and Hilary are talking to an audience, they normally ask plenty of questions that require the audience members to produce more than brief, confirmatory responses.

Bob: I sometimes ask light-hearted questions to create a fun atmosphere.

Hilary: I ask a lot of questions because the people in my audience enjoy answering questions.

Like Bob, you may sometimes want to ask one or two questions simply to get a laugh and generate a light-hearted moment. Like Hilary, you may like to ask questions because you recognize that your audience members

will enjoy the interactivity this produces.

However, most of your questions--the questions that call for significant audience involvement--will serve a more specific purpose and will be serious in nature.

Successful speakers ask demanding questions that call for a significant level of audience response. They might ask these questions if:
- the audience knows more than the speaker,
- they wish to determine the emotional state of the audience.

Question

You make a list to remind yourself of the times when you should ask questions to produce a significant audience response. What do you include on your list?

Options:

1. Ask questions to produce a fun atmosphere.

2. Ask questions when there are people in the audience who are better informed about a particular point.

3. Ask questions to determine the emotional condition of the audience.

4. Ask questions to allow the audience to enjoy some interactivity.

Answer:

Actually, you should ask questions when some of your audience members are more knowledgeable than you are on a point and when you need to learn the emotional state of the audience.

Option 1: This is an incorrect choice. Such questions do not produce a significant audience response. Instead, ask questions when you know the audience knows more than you or when you want to determine their emotional state.

Option 2: This is a correct choice. You can use questions to draw out the knowledge and expertise in your audience. This will help you support your presentation while also acknowledging the level of expertise in your audience.

Option 3: This is a correct choice. Ask the audience members how they feel about a particular issue, especially if negative emotions are involved. This way, you can understand and deal with their emotions directly.

Option 4: This choice is incorrect. While such questions may make the presentation enjoyable, they will not produce a significant response from the audience. Instead, ask questions that require considered responses.

How should you ask questions to benefit from the acquired knowledge of the people in your audience or discover their state of mind?

There are many occasions when Anna is happy to learn from her audience or when she needs to determine the emotional state of her audience.

Use expertise

"I utilize the expert knowledge in the audience by asking for very specific information or conclusions to supplement something I have said. I also ask for an expert to comment on something I have said. I do not ask a leading question."

Surface emotion

"To enable members of my audience to express their emotions, I tactfully ask them how they feel about an issue. This is particularly useful if negative feelings are involved."

Acknowledge emotion

"I comment sensitively and empathetically on the feelings that are revealed. For example, I might say: 'I understand why you feel strongly about this.'"

It is important for a speaker to use the expertise of the audience. However, you should not attempt to manipulate it by using a leading question such as, "I'm right, aren't I?"

If people are reluctant to reveal their feelings, you can ask a question to suggest how they may be feeling. For example, "Do you feel angry?" Having uncovered feelings, you cannot ignore them--you must respond with a sensitive comment.

It is helpful if you have a strategy for asking questions of your audience members. If you are trying to obtain information and discover feelings, you need to select appropriate questions that enable you to do this effectively and with sensitivity.

Case Study: Question 1 of 3
Scenario

You are the factory manager at Bulk Fabrication. The CEO has set new and challenging goals. You have some ideas about how to achieve the targets, so you gather your team of production supervisors to present your proposals to them and get their reactions.

Answer the questions that follow, in order, to show how you will ask your team questions during your presentation.

Question

The key to increasing production is getting more out of the assembly line. Unlike you, the production supervisors work on the assembly line every day, and you want to benefit from their knowledge. What questions do you ask?

Options:

1. "What actions could we take that would increase assembly line production?"

2. "A ten percent increase in production is certainly possible, isn't it?"

3. "Shall I tell you how we can increase production by ten percent?"

4. "I believe we could increase assembly line production by ten percent. Are there any reasons, based on levels of training or machine quality, that would prevent this?"

Answer:

To take advantage of the supervisors' knowledge, you need to ask for specific information. Use questions that call for expert comment on something you have said.

Option 1: This is a correct choice. You want to ask questions that show respect for what your audience knows. An open question like this is not leading and encourages the experts in the audience to give full, honest responses.

Option 2: This choice is incorrect. This is a leading question. Your audience members may resent being asked to agree with you. Instead, ask an open question that will allow them to give a full answer without feeling like they have to agree with you.

Option 3: This is an incorrect choice. This question isn't asking the experts in your audience to share anything. It's simply asking them to listen to you. Instead, ask a question that encourages them to share their opinions.

Option 4: This is a correct choice. This begins with a statement phrased as your opinion and follows with an open question that invites the audience to discuss the issue and share their expertise. This will encourage full, genuine answers.

Case Study: Question 2 of 3

The supervisors do not seem happy about the suggestion that they need to increase production, although they do not reveal their feelings directly. What questions could you ask about their state of mind?

Options:

1. "You seem unhappy. Do you feel the target is unreasonable?"

2. "How do you feel about the targets?"

3. "You're just miserable. What's your problem?"

4. "Don't you feel, like me, that these targets are achievable?"

Answer:

You can uncover the supervisors' emotional state in two ways: suggest how they may be feeling, or tactfully ask them to tell you how they feel.

Option 1: This is a correct choice. This question is tactful in asking the audience about their feelings on the issue. A good question conveys a sense of empathy and sensitivity to the issue and encourages people to express what they really think.

Option 2: This choice is correct. The tone of this question does not assume feelings one way or another and invites audience members to share their thoughts. This is a good way to open the floor for discussion.

Option 3: This is an incorrect choice. A good question about emotions must be tactful, and this question is not. Use a question that shows empathy and that conveys your sensitivity to your audience's feelings.

Option 4: This choice is incorrect. This question assumes the audience feels the same way you do. A good question will help the audience members express exactly how they feel. Otherwise, discussion on the issue will be closed and stilted.

Case Study: Question 3 of 3

The supervisors finally reveal their feelings. They are extremely discontented; they do not feel that anyone understands how hard they work to meet the existing targets. How do you respond?

Options:

1. I tell the supervisors that feeling unhappy won't help anyone, and they all need to focus on the new targets.

Giving Successful Presentations

2. I move rapidly to the next part of my presentation without commenting.

3. I tell the supervisors that their feelings are understandable, and I reassure them that they are doing a great job.

4. I tell the supervisors that everyone works hard, and they are no different than anyone else.

Answer:

You ought to comment sensitively and empathetically on the supervisors' state of mind.

Option 1: This is an incorrect choice. You should respond in a way that shows the supervisors you care about how they feel and understand where they're coming from. A response like this one lacks any empathy and will shut down the discussion.

Option 2: This choice is incorrect. Feelings that arise, however negative or uncomfortable, should be acknowledged and addressed. Comment directly on what has been said by expressing a sensitivity to the issue and empathizing with how they feel.

Option 3: This is the correct choice. You want to respond in a way that is sensitive to their feelings and that shows you care about how they feel. Never leave such honesty hanging without an empathetic response.

Option 4: This choice is incorrect. This response lacks empathy and has an insensitive tone. Respond to the supervisors more empathetically by saying you understand how they could feel that way.

The right thing to do--rather than simply presenting your proposals as a fait accompli--was to take positive advantage of the supervisors' detailed knowledge.

It is not surprising that the supervisors felt unappreciated, and you should have questioned them in a way that uncovered those negative feelings. You should have followed up with a sensitive, empathetic comment.

The expertise of your audience is a resource you can use. How people feel is important. Use questions to supplement your knowledge.

TAKING QUESTIONS FROM AN AUDIENCE

Taking questions from an audience

If your audience wants to ask you lots of questions, it's usually a very good sign. Be pleased. However, you need to know how to effectively manage the different types of questions your audience members will likely ask.

Brett is preparing for a presentation. He expects questions from his audience; he knows from experience that most questions belong to one of three types.

I am also frequently asked about things that, even though they may be interesting, are outside the scope of my talk and are irrelevant.

There will be questions from audience members who don't understand something I've already covered.

I will also be asked to say more about areas of content I have talked about.

Of book, sometimes there's a difficult person in the audience who asks an aggressive question or a question that is only designed to demonstrate the questioner's own knowledge. But this is really unusual. Most questioners are cooperative.

Question

You are an experienced public speaker. An inexperienced colleague asks for advice about questions. He wants to know the kinds of questions that speakers are commonly asked. What do you say to him?

Options:

1. "Often, the questioner wants you to clarify things you have already talked about."

2. "The questioner asks you a question because she wants you to say more about areas of content you have already mentioned."

3. "Often, the questioner will ask you an aggressive question."

4. "Questioners frequently ask a question designed to demonstrate their knowledge to the audience."

5. "Often, the questioner asks about something irrelevant that is outside the scope of the presentation."

Answer:

In fact, the common types of questions are questions for clarification, questions in which you are asked to add to what you have already said, and irrelevant questions.

Option 1: This is a correct choice. A common type of question is one that asks to clarify something covered in the presentation. Your colleague can expect to have questions like this.

Option 2: This choice is correct. If an audience member wants to know more about something that was not covered in detail, they may ask a question requesting more information. Your colleague will probably receive this kind of question.

Option 3: This is an incorrect choice. Although it's possible someone will ask this type of question, it's rare. More common questions include requests for clarification or for additional information on the content covered in the presentation.

Option 4: This choice is incorrect. While an occasional audience member may do this, it does not happen very often. Common questions will be to clarify a point or to request further discussion of some of the content covered in his presentation.

Option 5: This is a correct choice. Your colleague will probably get a question about something that is outside the topic he is covering in his presentation. They may be interesting topics, but they are clearly outside the scope of the presentation.

How should you respond to the questions that you are asked by your audience members?

No matter what kind of question you are asked and who asks it, two basic rules should govern your response. An effective response:

- shows respect for the questioner,
- is appropriate in the context of the presentation.

Question

You want to remind yourself of the fundamental rules that must always govern your response to questions, so you make a list. What do you include in your list?

Options:

1. I should show that I am more knowledgeable than the questioner.

2. I must give an answer to the question that would be satisfactory in any situation.

3. I should indicate that I respect the person asking the question.

4. I should make it clear that I like the questioner.

5. My answer must, within the limitations of the presentation situation, be appropriate.

Answer:

You should respond to questions by showing respect for the questioner and by providing an answer which is appropriate in the presentation situation.

Option 1: This choice is incorrect. A good response will show respect for the person asking the question. By trying to show that you are more knowledgeable, you are not showing respect to the questioner.

Option 2: This choice is incorrect. Your answer should be one that is appropriate for the particular context. You will need to evaluate what is appropriate for your situation, but usually an answer that is concise and helpful is best.

Option 3: This is a correct choice. A good response shows respect to the person asking the question. You should not act like the question was stupid or try to prove that you know more than the questioner. Listen respectfully and provide a response.

Option 4: This choice is incorrect. Your response demonstrates that you respect the questioner, which does not necessarily mean you like the person. Regardless of how you feel about the person, you show him respect.

Option 5: This choice is correct. When answering a question, take the context into consideration. Consider the subject you are talking about and how much time you can take to shape an appropriate response.

Giving Successful Presentations

How does a speaker establish a respectful relationship with the person who asks the question? And how does a speaker make sure that the answer is appropriate within the framework of the presentation?

Respectful

"When the question is asked, I show that I am listening. I also acknowledge the question once it has been asked."

Appropriate

"I provide a short answer. I also ensure that my answer helps the questioner."

There may be times during your presentation when the questioner interrupts you as you are speaking. Even in this case, you should still listen to and acknowledge the question.

Your answer should be brief because although the questioner is interested in your response, others may not be. In other words, a lengthy answer would act as a distraction in the context of the presentation.

Question

During a presentation training seminar, Noah noted the ways a speaker should respond to questions. Unfortunately, he now cannot remember which behaviors correspond to which of the two basic rules. Help Noah match each basic requirement to one or more of its attributes.

Options:

A. shows respect

B. is appropriate

Targets:

1. Your answer should be brief.
2. You must indicate that you have heard the question.

3. When the question is asked, you must make it clear that you are listening.

4. Your answer should be helpful to the questioner.

Answer:

You should show respect by listening to and then acknowledging the question. You should provide an appropriate answer, which means a brief and helpful one.

Keeping an answer brief and concise is a way of providing an appropriate response. Noah can give an appropriate response by taking the context and the time limitations into consideration.

Noah needs to show his audience members that he is listening to them. Acknowledging a question indicates he is listening and is a way of showing his audience respect.

If an audience member feels like Noah has not listened to his question, he may feel like Noah has acted disrespectfully. Noah should be careful to make it clear he is listening in order to show respect.

A good answer is one that is helpful. By providing an answer that helps the questioner, Noah is providing an appropriate response. Anything that is not helpful is inappropriate.

When an audience member asks a question during one of her presentations, Iris works hard to indicate her respect for the questioner by showing that she is listening. Then, as soon as the questioner stops speaking, she acknowledges the question.

listen

"I indicate, by using positive, affirming words and actions, that I am listening."

acknowledge

"I thank the questioner for the question, or I repeat the question to show that I have understood."

You show that you are listening by looking at the speaker, by nodding as the question is being asked, or by using words like "right," "OK," or "yes" as the question is being asked.

To acknowledge the question, thank the questioner for the question indirectly or use a positive comment such as, "That's an interesting question." You can repeat the question by reformulating it in your own words. The basic rules for responding effectively to questions are always the same. And you always show respect by using the same behaviors, no matter what the question.

However, the behaviors that constitute an appropriate answer depend on which of the three common kinds of questions you have been asked: a question for clarification, a request for more information, or an irrelevant question.

Once a question has been asked and she has acknowledged it, Iris provides a brief and helpful answer.

Clarification

"If the questioner asks for clarification about something I have said, I remind him of the relevant content by summarizing or spend a short time focusing in more detail on one aspect of the relevant content."

More information

"If the questioner wants additional information, I expand for not more than a minute on what I have already said. I then invite the questioner to contact me afterward if she is still curious."

Irrelevant

"If the question is off the subject, I politely point it, and then invite the questioner to contact me after the presentation."

Example:

Question 1: Clarifying

"An engineer didn't understand what I had said about how we solved the budget issues with the client."

Answer 1

"I found the relevant slide, brought it up on the screen, and touched on the main points again."

Question 2: Asking for more information

"One engineer asked me to speak more about the first phase of the project, in which we established relationships with subcontractors and government representatives."

Answer 2

"I gave him another little example of how we had built trust through a partnership approach with a subcontractor. Then I said, 'Look, it's hard to do justice to this in the time available. Why don't you come to my office tomorrow and we'll discuss it?'"

Question 3: Irrelevant question

"One engineer asked me about the shopping mall I worked on a couple of years ago. He wanted to know what lessons I had learned from that."

Answer 3

"I said that there were a lot of lessons from that project, but unfortunately they were outside the scope of my talk. I suggested that he might like to call me in the next week, and I'd be happy to talk about the shopping mall."

Carlos does a terrific job of handling the three questions. The first questioner didn't understand an area of content that had already been dealt with, and bringing the slide back up and going over the main points briefly was an appropriate way to handle this. Carlos did not allow himself to be distracted by the questioner who wanted to know more. Giving one case study and then inviting the individual to contact him later kept the presentation on track.

The third question had nothing to do with the presentation, and Carlos was right to courteously sidestep it by inviting the questioner to call him later for more information.

Case Study: Question 1 of 2

Scenario

When she presented the plans for the April promotion at Bronze Stores to her store managers, Diane was asked three questions.

General comments

"While the question was being asked, I checked my notes. In one case, it gave me a chance to find the right slide. Once the questioner stopped speaking, I always said, 'Thanks for asking the question,' or something similar."

Question 1

"Dawn was not sure what I had said about the point-of-sale material we'll be using, so she asked me to go over it again."

Answer 1

"She only wanted to know about the point-of-sale material that we've never used before, so I reminded her of what I had said earlier. It didn't take long."

Question 2

"One store manager asked me to add to what I had already said about the special role that her store was going to have in the promotion."

Answer 2

"She was very interested, so I produced a couple of handouts about her store, and we went through them for about ten minutes."

Question 3

"One guy knew we already had plans for the autumn promotion, and he asked about that."

Answer 3

"I said I was sorry, but the autumn promotion was not on the agenda. However, he was right, we do have plans. I said if he wanted to call me later in the week, I'd be happy to talk about them."

Question

How effectively does Diane respond to the questions she is asked?

Options:

1. She uses all the techniques to demonstrate respect to the questioners.

2. Diane uses some of the techniques for showing respect to the questioners.

3. Diane responds appropriately to Question 1 and the speaker who asks for clarification.

4. She responds appropriately to Question 2 and the speaker who wants additional information.

5. Diane responds appropriately to Question 3 and the speaker with the irrelevant question.

Answer:

Diane could have shown more respect toward her questioners, and she did not respond appropriately to the speaker who wanted additional information.

Option 1: Incorrect. Diane did not make eye contact with any of the questioners as they were asking their

Giving Successful Presentations

questions. Instead, she looked at her notes and slides. She also spent too much time responding to the question a special role for one store.

Option 2: This is a correct choice. Diane did thank each of the questioners for asking their questions. However, she did not make eye contact with any of them. Instead, she looked at her notes or slides while the others were talking.

Option 3: This is a correct choice. Diane did return to the material she had already covered and went over it again. She did not spend too much time lingering on it, and she did go back to the right point in her slides to review the material.

Option 4: This choice is incorrect. Diane spent 10 minutes responding, which was too long for the context and was an inappropriate response for that setting. Giving a brief answer and having the person contact her later would have been better.

Option 5: Correct. Although he asked a question outside the scope of her presentation, Diane responded respectfully. She politely explained that it was not the topic of her presentation and invited him to contact her later about the question.

Case Study: Question 2 of 2

How could Diane have responded more effectively to the questions she was asked by the managers?

Options:

1. She could have nodded, while making eye contact with the speaker, as the questions were being asked.

2. Diane might have indicated her interest in the questions by repeating them in her own words.

3. Diane could have indicated that she was interested in the questions by saying "right" or "yes" as they were being asked.

4. She should have spent less time answering the question from the manager who wanted additional information.

If the manager was not satisfied by the answer, Diane could have asked her to get in touch later.

5. Diane should have made some attempt to provide an answer to the irrelevant question.

Answer:

Diane could have shown more respect for the speakers through affirmative actions and words. She should also have responded briefly to the manager who wanted additional information but invited later contact.

Option 1: This choice is correct. Diane did not make eye contact with any of the people asking questions. She could have done a better job by looking at them while they were asking their questions and nodding to show she was listening.

Option 2: Correct choice. Although not always necessary, Diane could have demonstrated that she understood the questions before launching into her responses. A good way to demonstrate your understanding is to repeat the question asked.

Option 3: This is a correct choice. Diane didn't give any confirmation of her interest as the questions were being asked. She could have shown she was really hearing the question by using affirming words while questions were being asked.

Option 4: Correct. Spending 10 minutes on the response for this question was too long. Others probably were not interested in the answer, so keeping the response concise would have shown more respect for the rest of the audience.

Option 5: Incorrect. Diane handled the irrelevant question appropriately. The best way to respond is to explain that the question is outside the scope of the presentation and then invite the questioner to contact you later for discussion.

Diane did a good job in a number of ways. However, although she thanked her questioners for their questions once they had finished, she did not react in any positive, affirming way as they were speaking, which would have shown greater respect.

Also, she didn't handle the questioner who asked for additional information well--she forgot to keep her answer brief. Respond effectively to questions by always applying the same basic rules. Formulate appropriate answers according to each of the three common question types.

SECTION 2 - DEALING WITH QUESTIONS DURING YOUR PRESENTATION

SECTION 2 - Dealing with Questions during Your Presentation

Many presenters believe that their job is to talk, and the audience's job is to listen. Questions from the audience? No, thank you. Does this describe you? The members of your audience are interested in what you're saying, so they want a chance to ask you questions about your presentation.

A speaker will usually set aside a period of time at the end of her presentation for the audience to ask questions. A question-and-answer session at the end of your speech provides a great opportunity for interaction, but how do you ensure that it is successful?

A rhetorical question is a device used by a speaker to command attention; it does not need a direct response. A speaker also often asks questions to check audience understanding; she'll say, "Is that clear?" or "OK?" This type of question only calls for a limited audience response.

On the other hand, questions that demand a direct and substantial audience response stimulate significant audience involvement in the presentation.

If your audience wants to ask you lots of questions, it's usually a very good sign. Be pleased. However, you need to know how to effectively manage the different types of questions your audience members will likely ask.

USING VISUAL AIDS

Using visual aids

You probably already use visual aids to support your presentations. But do you use visual aids for the right reasons and in the right way? Amy and Omar both have viewpoints about the place of visual aids in presentations.

Amy: I always use lots of slides. It's easy. I have my presentations stored in my computer, and I can retrieve them any time I want.

Omar: I've sat through many boring presentations with speakers who have dozens of slides. You could walk out of the room, and the speaker wouldn't even notice. I've learned my lesson: Never use visuals.

Amy and Omar are both wrong. The effective use of visual aids has real benefits. But if you overuse them or ignore them completely, you don't get those benefits.

Jim makes a lot of sales presentations, and most of the time he uses visual backup. He is well aware that if used properly, visual aids give him an advantage.

Emphasis

"Using slides is a way to emphasize my message. I tell the audience my message, and my slides repeat it in visual form."

Accuracy

"Using slides helps me ensure that I thoroughly cover the content of my presentation and that I don't leave anything out."

Reminder

"I often give my audience written handouts to take away. They serve as a reminder of my presentation and my message."

Question

Some of your team members don't make good use of visual support in their presentations. What do you say to persuade them of the benefits of knowing how to make the most of visual aids?

Options:

1. "Visual aids mean you have to work less at developing your relationship with your audience."

2. "They are a way of emphasizing your message as you speak."

3. "Using visual aids means you can include as much information as you want in your presentation."

4. "Using slides ensures that you cover the content fully, omitting nothing."

5. "Visual aids in the form of handouts will help the audience to remember your presentation."

Answer:

In fact, using visuals emphasizes your message and ensures that you cover the content completely. Handouts serve as a permanent reminder of your presentation.

Option 1: This is an incorrect choice. It is still necessary to develop a good relationship with the audience. Otherwise, the audience may feel ignored. Using slides will also help with emphasis, accuracy, and remembering what you said.

Option 2: This choice is correct. The slides can be used to repeat what you have said, which emphasizes your point. This way, the audience receives the message twice rather than just once.

Option 3: This is an incorrect choice. Using slides does not mean you can cram more into a presentation, but they will help you not leave out anything important. However, you should still keep your presentation concise.

Option 4: This choice is correct. Slides can help your team members remember the content they wanted to cover. That way, they don't leave anything out and are sure to cover the content in full.

Option 5: This choice is correct. If the audience has visual aids they can take with them, they will be better able to recall the material. If your team members use visual aids as hand outs, they are aiding their audience's ability to remember.

Visual aids have terrific benefits, provided they are used in the right form, to the right extent, and at the right time.

TYPES OF VISUAL AIDS

Types of visual aids

What are the main types of visual aids? And when are they best used? Elena gives many successful presentations. How does she use visual aids?

I often use slides. I project them onto a screen behind me.

I also find that a flip chart or white board I can write on is very helpful in some situations.

The other kind of visual I frequently use is printed handouts.

Slides projected onto a screen, flip charts, white boards, and handouts are the most common types of visual aids used in business presentations. If used correctly, they provide support for the speaker and the audience at the same time.

Elena occasionally uses two other types of visual aids, but she is aware of their limitations.

Elena will occasionally show a video to introduce variety into a training session or a day-long conference.

When she has no other option, she relies on speaker's notes on cards or a piece of paper.

Video

"Video replaces the speaker. It does not support him or her."

Notes

"Notes provide support for the speaker, but they do not help the audience in any way."

Question

You want to brief your team about how to use visual aids. You have made a list of common types of visuals that support the audience and the speaker. What visual aids are on your list?

Options:

1. flip charts and white boards
2. video
3. slides projected onto a screen
4. speaker's notes
5. handouts

Answer:

The most common types of visual aids are slides, flip charts, white boards, and handouts. Video and speaker's notes are sometimes useful, but they do not assist both the speaker and the audience.

Option 1: This is a correct choice. Flip charts and white boards are visual aids you and your team members will use often. These media are good for brainstorming and for writing down ideas that come out of the meeting.

Option 2: This is an incorrect choice. Video often replaces the speaker. Your team will want aids that support their presentations, not media that replaces them as the speaker. Video should be used rarely and only for specific purposes.

Option 3: This choice is correct. Slides are perhaps the most common visual aid used. Using slides will make you and your team appear professional, as your presentation is well-prepared with the content ready and polished.

Option 4: This choice is incorrect. Notes are very helpful for a speaker because they help the presenter remember what he wants to cover. However, notes provide no benefit to the audience and are not a visual aid for presentations.

Option 5: Correct choice. Handouts are also common for presenters to use. Handouts are good for helping the audience remember the content after your presentation.

It is important to know how to effectively use each common type of visual aid.

As a vice-president for Moregas Industrial Gases, Reuben's work is varied. He manages a team and also has a lot of client contact, so he finds that he needs to employ three common types of visual aids.

Slides

"I use slides when it is important to impress the audience with the professionalism of my preparation and all aspects of the delivery. Projecting slides onto a screen is also necessary in a large venue."

Flip chart

"For small audiences and informal situations, writing notes on flip charts and white boards is a great way to use visual aids."

Handouts

"I can refer to handouts during the presentation; this can be helpful when the content is complex. I often distribute handouts at the end of the presentation as a record of the content."

It is important to use slides appropriately. When Reuben makes a presentation to clients, he always makes sure that he creates a favorable impression by using high-quality slides. He would never scribble notes on a flip chart. On the other hand, he makes extensive use of the white board in his regular, informal team meetings. Handouts may be distributed at the end as a record of the presentation. For example, Reuben handed out brochures after his last client presentation.

Question

Julia is confused. She has some upcoming presentations, and she has asked her colleagues for advice about when to use different types of visual aids. Unfortunately, their advice is contradictory. Which advice should she follow?

Options:

1. "You should refer to handouts during your presentation if the presentation material is particularly complex."

2. "Use slides when you are speaking in a large hall, or when your presentation has to create an impression of well-prepared professionalism."

3. "Use a white board or flip chart when the presentation content is particularly complicated."

4. "You could distribute handouts at the end as a record of your presentation."

5. "You should use a flip chart or white board when you're talking to a few people in a relaxed environment."

6. "Slides are good when you need to encourage lots of audience participation during the presentation."

Giving Successful Presentations

Answer:

Handouts provide a permanent record or a reference for complicated content. Slides, on the other hand, create an impression of well-prepared professionalism, and a white board is good for interactive, informal situations.

Option 1: This is a correct choice. Handouts can be particularly helpful if Julia's content is complex. The handouts allow her audience to refer to the material and make notes, and they will help the audience remember the content after the presentation.

Option 2: This choice is correct. If the audience is large, projecting content on a screen allows all of Julia's audience to see her presentation. The slides also create a professional image since Julia will look well-prepared.

Option 3: This is an incorrect choice. White boards or flip charts are not helpful when the content is complex. Handouts are more helpful because the audience can keep a record of the content and can make notes for themselves.

Option 4: Correct choice. The audience can take handouts with them after the presentation is over to help them remember the content. Julia should distribute these at the end so people listen to her instead of reading the handouts.

Option 5: This choice is correct. White boards and flip charts are good for Julia to use with a smaller audience and a more informal setting. They are great for brainstorming or capturing ideas and are easy for everyone in a small group to see.

Option 6: This choice is incorrect. White boards and flip charts would be better if Julia wants lots of interaction.

Sorin Dumitrascu

Slides are better if Julia is presenting to a large audience or needs to project a professional, well-prepared image.

Visual aids can provide tremendous support for your presentation if you choose the right type or combination.

IMPROVING PRESENTATIONS

Improving presentations

Many presenters abuse visual aids. This topic shows you how you can make effective use of visuals and enhance the quality of your presentations.

Celeste and Danny use visuals incorrectly, but for very different reasons.

Celeste: I always make extensive use of slides and handouts. I think that's what my audiences expect.

Danny: I never use slides or handouts. I don't have time to produce them. I might quickly write a few notes on a flip chart if it's absolutely necessary, but I avoid using visual aids as much as possible.

Celeste makes the basic mistake of allowing her visual aids to dominate the presentation. Successful presenters make sure that their visuals support their message but remain secondary to the speaker.

If your presentation will benefit from visual aids, you should use them. Danny is only interested in his own convenience. If his presentation needs visuals, he must find the time to produce them.

Sorin Dumitrascu

Question

You are producing a slide for a training workshop on presentations. The title of the visual is "How to Use Visual Aids Effectively." Which of the following bullet points would you include on your slide?

Options:

1. Dominate the speaker
2. Never use if it can be avoided
3. Remain secondary to the speaker
4. Support the presentation message
5. Always use if they will benefit the presentation

Answer:

Visual aids should remain secondary to the speaker, but provide effective support for his message. They should always be used if they help the presentation.

Option 1: This choice is incorrect. When visual aids dominate the speaker, they are being misused. Instead, visual aids should be used to support the speaker meaning they are secondary to the speaker and support the message.

Option 2: This is an incorrect choice. Never using visual aids is an extreme over-correction for bad use. Visual aids can be useful and should be used if they will benefit the presentation. They remain secondary to the speaker and support the message.

Option 3: This choice is correct. Visual aids should not dominate the presentation. Instead, they should be secondary to the presenter. Visual aids can prompt what you say but are not a script for you to read from.

Option 4: This is a correct choice. Visual aids can provide great support for a message and should be used when they benefit the presentation. Overusing or under using visual aids can lead to a lack of support for your message.

Option 5: This is a correct choice. Some speakers make the mistake of not using visual aids at all. You should not make that same mistake. Use visual aids any time they will benefit your presentation but do not let them dominate.

The types of visual aids that you will use most frequently during presentations are slides, a white board or flip chart, and handouts.

How should you use each of these visual aids so that the visual remains secondary but still supports your message?

Nancy is a marketing manager and experienced presenter who makes effective use of all three common types of visual aids in her presentations.

Slides

"The text on my slides is a prompt for me, not a script to read. Slides also enable me to present statistical information concisely, as powerful visual images."

Flip chart

"The flip chart and white board provide the basis for collaborative interaction with the audience."

Handouts

"I use handouts in my presentations to clarify material."

Question

Vera, your colleague, is trying to make sure she understands when and how to use each type of visual aid. The visual aids and the guidelines are shown. Help her match each type of visual aid with one or more of the guidelines that apply to its use.

Options:

A. slides

B. notes on a flip chart or white board

C. handouts referred to during the presentation

Targets:

1. prompt the presenter; they should not be read word for word

2. are used to clarify content

3. are a good way to present statistical information concisely

4. provide collaborative interaction with the audience

Answer

In fact, handouts should be used to clarify points for the audience. Flip chart notes are constructed with the help of the audience. Slides are not a script, they are a prompt; they are also used to project powerful visual images.

Slides provide content outlines that are excellent for prompting the presenter. However, Vera should not read those slides as if they were a script. The slides should remain secondary to her as the presenter.

If the content is complex, handouts can be an excellent way to clarify the information for the audience. Vera's audience can make notes on the handouts and keep them for later reference.

Charts, tables, and other visual representations of statistical information can be displayed concisely and effectively through slides. Slides allow Vera to project these powerful images for everyone to see and understand.

If Vera wants the audience to interact or collaborate, flip charts and white boards are a good choice. She can use these to generate ideas, take notes, and brainstorm with her audience.

So now you know the basic principles you should follow to use the potential of three types of visual aids. But how should you put those principles into practice?

Giving Successful Presentations

Nancy often uses slides to support her highly effective marketing presentations to colleagues in other departments. Slides can have text and graphic elements.

Text

"I use a small number of text slides with a few bullet points on each slide. Fifty words per slide is the maximum. I talk about the points on the slides, rather than reading them to the audience. In this way, the slides act as a prompt for me."

Graphics

"I use figures, such as graphs and pie charts, to communicate information in a compressed form. I use a figure to demonstrate a point I have made or to introduce information that I am about to discuss."

Speakers often have too many slides and too much information on each slide. Their presentations consist of reading the text on their slides from the screen. Instead of doing this, follow Nancy's advice. Use a small number of slides, and create them yourself. Do not take figures from a printed source and insert them into your presentation. If you have to use a table from a printed source, highlight the key information on the slide.

Nancy recently made good use of the white board during an extremely interactive meeting with her team about a new marketing campaign. In another presentation, she used handouts in the form of the completed proposal for a campaign.

white board

"I write the notes during the presentation. They are a combination of audience ideas and my ideas. They are the result of discussion in the group."

handouts

"We only read or refer to short sections from the handouts during the presentation. I answer questions and add information about those sections."

Alan, the owner of Boatsforall, met with his design team to discuss the development of a new, affordable small yacht. He used a flip chart in this meeting.

He then gave a presentation to all of his employees about the company's plans. He referred to his report: "Boatsforall: The Next Five Years."

Design team

"I wrote down a few basic headings, such as Materials, Performance Criteria, and so on. I talked about them and added the team's thoughts to the flip chart notes. By the end of the afternoon, we had organized a basic blueprint."

All employees

"I added details to parts of the report that affected certain groups, and I answered questions. It was necessary to read a few statements out loud, but not many. It was a long report, so I made sure that people had a copy in advance."

Alan developed his notes on the flip chart during his presentation, which was good. If you need to prepare notes in advance, then you should use slides. His own initial notes were very short and were used to stimulate audience ideas, which were then added to the flip chart-- through collaborative interaction.

Alan did not make the mistake of reading or discussing large parts of the report. He clarified it by directing attention to small sections he wanted to talk about, and answering questions from the audience. If you are using a lengthy handout, the audience should either read it in advance or take it away for future reference.

Giving Successful Presentations

Case Study: Question 1 of 2
Scenario

Pablo recently gave several presentations using visual aids: one about financial performance to senior management, one about possible new training initiatives to the team he manages, and the third, based on his report "Trends in HR," to the whole department.

Pablo's team

"I started with a blank white board. I wrote down the names of new seminars I think we should develop next year. As we discussed the possible structure and content of each one, I added notes to the white board."

Whole department

"I distributed the 30-page report at the start of the presentation. I read the most interesting sections of the report out loud, commenting on them as I read."

Senior management

"I used fewer than ten slides, with a few notes on each about one aspect of the financial results. I discussed the points, adding detail to the information on the slide.

I also used slides showing spreadsheets about attendance and pass rates to show that there has been some improvement. I copied the spreadsheets from the annual report."

Question

How effective was Pablo in using slides, handouts, and the white board in his presentations?

Options:

1. Pablo used text slides well.

2. He made good use of slides to present statistical information.

3. Pablo used handouts well.

4. He made good use of the flip chart.

Answer:

In fact, Pablo used text slides and the flip chart well. He did not make good use of handouts or slides with statistical data.

Option 1: This is a correct choice. When Pablo presented to the senior management, he used fewer than 10 slides and did not read directly from them. He added to the slides and used them mostly as prompts.

Option 2: This is an incorrect choice. While Pablo did use slides to present statistical information, he displayed spreadsheets. Better use of the slides would have been to display graphical representations of the data instead of just spreadsheets.

Option 3: This is an incorrect choice. Pablo used handouts poorly. He distributed them at the beginning of his presentation to the whole department. The audience would have read those instead of listening to him. He also read directly from them.

Option 4: This choice is correct. Pablo chose to use the flip chart in the smaller team setting where he wanted collaboration. The team used that visual aid for developing and refining their ideas.

Case Study: Question 2 of 2

How could Pablo have made better use of his visual aids?

Options:

1. Pablo should have highlighted on his slides the parts of the spreadsheets he wanted to discuss.

2. He should have distributed the report to people in the department before the presentation and answered their questions during his presentation.

Giving Successful Presentations

3. Before the presentation, he should have written his detailed notes on the white board.

4. Pablo should not have read large parts of the report.

5. Pablo should have had more information about the quarterly results on his slides.

6. He could have produced his own slides about attendance and pass rates, rather than using pages from a report.

Answer:

Pablo should have distributed his report in advance because of its length, and he should not have read much of it aloud. He should either have prepared his own statistical slides or highlighted the relevant parts.

Option 1: This is a correct choice. A spreadsheet full of data can be overwhelming. By highlighting the important parts, Pablo can direct his audience's attention to what he wants to focus on. This will also help them remember the information.

Option 2: Correct. Pablo's audience was probably reading the handouts instead of listening to him. Since the handout was so big, giving it out in advance would give them time to read it and then have their questions answered during the presentation.

Option 3: This is an incorrect choice. White boards are not good for detailed notes. Detailed notes are best presented in slides or in a handout. White boards are better for simple notes where more input can be added by the audience.

Option 4: This is a correct choice. A visual aid is there as support for the speaker and message, not in lieu of them. By reading parts of the report, Pablo let it dominate the presentation. He could have handed it out earlier and commented on important parts.

Option 5: This choice is incorrect. Pablo included too much information on the quarterly reports. He needed to condense the statistical information to a more concise graphical representation to help his audience understand.

Option 6: This is a correct choice. Pablo let the visual aids dominate his presentation by reading straight from an already finished report. He should have created his own slides and then used the report for support.

It was good that Pablo only had a small number of slides and that he used them as a prompt, rather than a script. However, using spreadsheets in the way he did indicated that he had not given any thought to the concise presentation of data to an audience.

Reading pages from a report out loud to an audience is the worst way to use a handout. The handout, rather than the speaker, dominated the presentation. Pablo should have focused on and discussed short, relevant sections.

Remember, visual aids will only support your presentation if you use them in the right way. They are there to serve you, the speaker, and they should not dominate the presentation.

COMPUTER-AIDED SLIDES

Computer-aided slides

The computer adds a wonderful, new dimension to the presenter's art. You can produce your own slides, achieving professional-quality animations, artwork, and sound.

However, the power of presentation software should be used with caution.

Kristina now makes good use of slides in her presentations. In the past, however, she was fascinated by the obvious attractions of computer-aided presentations, and she made mistakes.

Mistake 1

"I tried to use a complete presentation that a colleague sent me, but it didn't work for me. I also gave a presentation without rehearsing the slides."

Mistake 2

"I used to incorporate all the complicated effects the software could produce."

If you intend to use slides that a colleague has prepared for his presentation, you must select from--and adapt-- the slides before using them for your presentation.

Delivering a computer-aided presentation is not difficult. However, you should rehearse thoroughly. Add and remove slides until you are comfortable and confident.

Most presentation software can produce powerful effects. This doesn't mean you have to incorporate all of them. You should select simple effects that serve your purpose. Do not use complex effects simply to demonstrate your fluency with the software.

Question

Your friend Russell has just started giving computer-aided presentations, and he is very enthusiastic about the technology. Because of your experience as a presenter, he asks you how it should be used. What do you say?

Options:

1. "Do not try to use all the effects the software is capable of. Use simple effects, only to the extent you need them."

2. "If someone sends you presentation slides, always modify the slides to suit yourself before using them."

3. "Use the full resources of the software to demonstrate your skill."

4. "Rehearse by using your slides until you are comfortable with the technology."

5. "If a colleague sends you presentation slides, do not alter the slides before using them."

Answer:

If a colleague sends you presentation slides, you should adapt them before using them. Always rehearse

Giving Successful Presentations

thoroughly with your slides, and do not use more effects than you actually need.

Option 1: This is a correct choice. Presentation software has all kinds of bells and whistles that may not necessarily contribute to the presentation. Russell should select only what will enhance his message.

Option 2: This is a correct choice. Russell's presentations should be accurately geared to his content, audience, and objective. He should modify slides someone else sends him to make sure he gives an effective presentation.

Option 3: This is an incorrect choice. Using all the resources of the software will not demonstrate skill with the subject, only the software. Instead, Russell should select what enhances his message for a more professional, considered impression.

Option 4: This choice is correct. Presenters often make the mistake of not rehearsing their slides. Russell should practice his slides so he gives the impression of being prepared and polished. He should never use slides without reviewing them.

Option 5: This is an incorrect choice. Russell's colleague may have used the slides for an entirely different purpose and audience. Russell will need to select what works for him, so his presentation is as effective as possible.

Your slides should make appropriate use of a variety of simple, computer-aided effects to:
- emphasize key moments,
- indicate structure.

Kristina gives many important sales presentations. It helps her to know how to use computer-aided slides to emphasize key moments and indicate structure.

Key moments

"I use effects that draw attention to the really important information that I want the audience to remember. I also use computer-aided effects to jolt the audience into giving a response."

Structure

"I use computer-aided effects to define the relationship between areas of text on an individual slide--and also to define the relationship between different slides."

Because Kristina uses minimal computer-aided effects to achieve specific goals, the effects she uses are more noticeable and effective.

Question

Russell knows that using computer-aided effects can really help his presentations, but he is not sure how he should use them. What do you say to him?

Options:

1. "You should use computer-aided effects to prevent your audience from becoming bored."

2. "You can use effects to highlight a significant fact that you want the audience to remember."

3. "You should use computer-aided effects to signal the relationship between different areas of text on a slide."

4. "Certain effects help when you want to force the audience into a sudden response."

5. "You should use effects produced with the help of a computer to speed up your presentation."

6. "You can use effects to indicate the relationship between different slides."

Answer:

Use computer-aided effects to show the structure of text on a slide or between slides. Use effects to force the audience into a response or draw attention to something significant at key moments.

Option 1: This choice is incorrect. The purpose of computer-aided effects is not to entertain the audience. Russell should use these effects to emphasize key moments, jolt the audience into a response, or highlight relationships in the content.

Option 2: This is a correct choice. Computer-aided effects can be used to draw attention to an important fact. If used well, the effect will stand out and help Russell's audience remember the fact.

Option 3: This choice is correct. Certain effects will help Russell signal relationships between different parts of a slide. In these instances, the effects will help the audience easily understand the content.

Option 4: This is a correct choice. Russell may want to grab his audience's attention at a certain point. In these instances, a computer-aided effect can help him create enough contrast to jolt his audience into taking particular note.

Option 5: This is an incorrect choice. Computer-aided effects should not drive his presentation. Russell should use these effects to emphasize key moments, jolt the audience into a response, or highlight relationships in the content.

Option 6: This choice is correct. Russell can help his audience understand how content on different slides relates through the efficient use of effects. This helps the audience understand the structure of his presentation.

Your presentation software gives you many effects to choose from. Which effects work best to highlight important moments or draw attention to structure?

Linda knows when to use slide effects that the audience will notice. She also knows how to choose the right effect for key moments or to stress structure.

Emphasis

"I highlight an important fact by animating a word, a phrase, or a number. I do not use sound effects for this purpose."

Structure of slide

"I build text on the slide in two ways. If the bullet points deal with an evolving story or process that needs detailed comment, I build them one at a time. If the bullet points are detail or an introduction and only require brief comment, I add them all at once."

Response

"I use photographs or cartoon images to provoke a strong emotional response, such as shock or laughter. The emotional response has to be integral to the presentation, not just gratuitous. Occasionally I use a relevant sound effect."

New section

"I indicate the structure of my presentation by the way I move from one slide to another. I make an immediate transition between most slides, but when a slide introduces a new main point, I make a slow transition, which takes a second or so."

Animated effects, such as the one on this page, are very noticeable. They are sufficient on their own to draw attention to the key information you want the audience to remember. Sound effects may distract from the information.

Amanda Toby is the CEO of Toby's Outdoor Furniture. She just finished making a presentation about her company at an international conference. She structured her presentation with great care, integrating a number of important, key moments and supporting it with computer-aided slides.

emphasis

"Toby's is 100 years old. I started off with a slide showing 25, then 50, then 75, and finally 100. The size of the numbers increased with each slide. My daughter wanted me to use a 'Happy Birthday' sound effect, but I refused. That would be overdoing it."

response

"I was talking about the traditions of Toby's. I had a slide with a photo of my grandfather, who started the business. People laughed because he looked kind of funny in his strange, old-fashioned clothes. But it was sympathetic laughter."

structure of slide

"I used a slide to introduce our new product line. I wanted to talk in detail about each product, so I built up the slide one bullet point at a time, starting with the title: New Product Line."

a new section

"I used four slides in the first part of the talk. When I finished with one slide, I brought in the next one directly. When I moved on to the second section, I melted one slide into the other--it took a second or two."

It sounds as though Amanda did a great job with her slides. The age of the company was something that she wanted people to remember, and her animation achieved this. She didn't make the mistake of employing a distracting sound effect. The photograph of her grandfather generated a strong emotional response and was highly relevant.

By introducing slides at the beginning of a new section in a different way, she drew attention to the structure. She built up the slide on the new product line using one bullet at a time, which suited the fact that she wanted to talk in detail about each product.

Case Study: Question 1 of 2
Scenario

You work for Perfecto Coffee Makers. You give a presentation to the management about how the market has received Numero Uno, Perfecto's new espresso machine.

Answer the questions that follow to show how you use computer-aided slides to enhance your presentation.

Question

Your presentation is carefully structured to communicate how the public has responded to the espresso machine. You indicate this structure through your use of computer-aided slides from the first section of your presentation, which deals with Numero Uno's performance over the first month. How do you do this?

Options:

1. There is no break between most slides; by dissolving the final slide, I slow the transition to the first slide of the second section.

2. On the slide describing one customer's experience over the month, I build the bullet points one by one, commenting on each.

3. I build in a one-second transition between each slide by dissolving from one slide to another.

4. When commenting briefly on regions where the machine is available, I show the slide all at once.

5. On the slide that lists the regions where the Numero Uno is available, I comment briefly and bring each bullet point in individually.

Answer:

In fact, the slides in your computer-aided presentation should be used to draw attention to the structural relationship between the slides and the text on individual slides.

Option 1: This is a correct choice. By using a slow transition between sections, you indicate a shift from one main point to the next. However, by keeping the quick transitions between the slides within a section, you indicate that they are related.

Option 2: This is a correct choice. Because the customer's experience evolves over time, it's a good choice to introduce the elements one bullet at a time. This gives the same effect as the story itself evolving over time.

Option 3: This choice is incorrect. Noticeable transitions should occur only between sections, not at the end of each slide. Transitions that stand out will signal a shift for your audience. Related slides should be connected through quick transitions.

Option 4: This is a correct choice. When there is no need to let information build over time, it can be presented all at once. Otherwise, it would slow down the presentation and emphasize the content incorrectly.

Option 5: This choice is incorrect. You want the audience to get a general overview. There is no need for you to let a story develop, so bringing up bullets individually is a mismatch for the content. Instead, introduce the information all at once.

Case Study: Question 2 of 2

You emphasize key moments in your presentation through your use of computer-aided slides. How do you do this?

Options:

1. I introduce the sales figures--which I really want the managers to remember--in the form of an animated graphic, which flies in from the left of the slide and then gets larger.

2. I amuse the managers with cartoon images of ducks praising the qualities of the Numero Uno espresso machine.

3. To enthuse the managers about public response to the Numero Uno, I show images of smiling and satisfied cafe owners using their new espresso machines.

4. I emphasize the number of orders for the Numero Uno with a blast of trumpet music and a graphic effect showing several trumpeters.

Answer:

You use your computer-aided slides to direct attention to key information you need the audience to remember and also to generate an emotional response.

Option 1: This is a correct choice. Animations are excellent for emphasizing an important figure, word, or phrase. If you really want your audience to remember something, animation is a good effect. However, be sure not to overuse animation.

Option 2: This is an incorrect choice. Images should be used to elicit a specific emotional response from the audience, not entertain them. They will not appreciate gratuitous graphics. Use graphics to enhance your message.

Option 3: Correct. In this instance, you are using graphics that support your message. The pictures are directly relevant to your presentation and your audience. They will also help you elicit a positive emotional response from the audience.

Option 4: Incorrect. The graphic and sound of trumpets has nothing to do with the number of orders for the machine. Graphics and sound should be relevant to the message. Animation is a good way to emphasize a point, but it should be relevant.

It was important to use computer-aided slides effectively--for example, to structure the introduction of content on the slide about the user of the Numero Uno and to separate the first section of your presentation from the others.

The simple but powerful and relevant effects produced also helped the managers to remember the sales figures and respond to the positive emotions of users of the machine.

If used poorly or overused, computer-generated effects will be a distraction. If used well, they will enhance your message.

SECTION 3 - EFFECTIVE TEAM PRESENTATIONS

SECTION 3 - Effective Team Presentations

Preparing and delivering a presentation on your own probably seems like enough of a challenge--you don't need the added complication of working with other people. There are times when, instead of presenting solo, you should speak as part of a team. But how do you know when to do so? If you make the wrong decision, your presentation will suffer.

You can't prepare for a team presentation the same way you would if you were presenting alone. Like any other situation in which you're working closely with a group of other people, you need to coordinate your efforts. You are part of a team presentation. One of your colleagues is speaking to the audience. What should you be doing? Delivering a convincing team presentation requires each team member to act as though he really is part of a team--throughout the entire presentation.

MAKING TEAM PRESENTATIONS

Making team presentations

Preparing and delivering a presentation on your own probably seems like enough of a challenge--you don't need the added complication of working with other people.

Perhaps you feel like Tom. Tom is not enthusiastic about the idea of presenting as part of a team.

It sounds like a lot of hassle to me.

I don't know anything about team presentations, and I hope I never have to find out.

In some speaking situations, a team effort is required. You should have a positive attitude about this--rather than a negative attitude like Tom's--because there are a number of benefits to presenting as part of a team.

Lucy often works with other people on her project team in presentation situations. She enjoys it and understands that it can be preferable to presenting on her own.

creativity

"For one thing, working as part of a team is certainly more stimulating and creative at the planning stage."

confidence

"I feel more confident because of the support I get from colleagues."

audience interest

"The audience is more interested because of the variety involved with having several speakers."

Question

You take Tom aside and tell him about the benefits of a team presentation situation. What do you say?

Options:

1. "You'll feel more confident as part of a team."

2. "Being part of a team reduces the amount of time you need to spend preparing your presentation."

3. "Being part of a team is a more creative and stimulating way to plan a presentation."

4. "A team presentation situation gives you a chance to demonstrate how good your speaking skills are compared to those of your colleagues."

5. "The level of audience interest is greater because of the variety that comes from having more than one speaker."

Answer:

Being part of a team is a more creative and stimulating way to plan; you'll feel more confident with the support of others; and the variety encourages a higher level of audience interest.

Option 1: This is a correct choice. Tom will get support from his fellow presenters when he presents as part of a team. This will help him feel more confident about the presentation.

Option 2: This is an incorrect choice. The amount of time required for planning will not be reduced. However, the level of creativity increases because of the

Giving Successful Presentations

collaborative planning process and produces a better final product.

Option 3: This is a correct choice. Working with a team is a collaborative process. During the planning stages, more people are involved and are sharing ideas, which makes the process more creative and stimulating.

Option 4: This is an incorrect choice. A team presentation actually provides the audience with more variety in presentation styles, which they will appreciate. It's a good chance for Tom to work with others and produce a quality presentation.

Option 5: This is a correct choice. Tom will find that the audience enjoys team presentations because it's not the same person talking the entire time. The variety afforded by team presentations will keep things interesting.

Working to create a successful presentation as part of a team should be a welcome opportunity.

CIRCUMSTANCES THAT REQUIRE A TEAM PRESENTATION

Circumstances that require a team presentation

There are times when, instead of presenting solo, you should speak as part of a team. But how do you know when to do so? If you make the wrong decision, your presentation will suffer.

Michelle and Travis were not impressed with the speakers who presented to them. Follow along as they describe these poor presentations.

Michelle: A team of three showed up to make a sales presentation. One of them did almost all the speaking, and frankly, the contributions of his two colleagues were of no value.

Travis: We had the opposite situation. We expected to hear from the heads of production and the chief financial officer, not just the CEO. It was really a waste of our time.

A team presentation is preferable in the following situations:

- A collective effort would be stronger than an individual one.

Giving Successful Presentations

- A team presentation suits the audience.

Question

The members of a small project team come to see you. They work closely as a team and would like to carry this aspect over to their presentations, but they are not sure when a team presentation is appropriate. What do you say to them?

Options:

1. "Make a team presentation when it suits the venue."

2. "Present as a team when doing so will produce a stronger presentation."

3. "Make a team presentation when this suits the audience."

4. "Make a team presentation when you have several strong speakers available."

Answer:

In fact, a team presentation is preferred if it suits the audience or if it will be more powerful as a result.

Option 1: This choice is incorrect. A team presentation is good when it suits the audience. The other criterion for doing a team presentation is when a collective effort would be stronger than a solo presentation.

Option 2: This choice is correct. If the presentation would be more powerful with multiple people presenting, then a team presentation is a good choice. However, if it weakens the presentation, then use a solo presenter approach.

Option 3: This is a correct choice. The audience may be expecting or wanting to hear from multiple people. In this case, a team presentation is appropriate. The project team should research audience expectations in advance.

Option 4: This choice is incorrect. The decision to make a team presentation depends on who the audience expects to hear from and whether other presenters would add any value. A solo presentation might be a better choice.

Grace is a highly experienced speaker who enjoys presenting and has no trouble captivating an audience, but there are occasions when she makes a team presentation because that's the correct choice for the audience.

Audience request

"Sometimes your audience members have requested that they want to hear from a team, not just one representative."

Audience expectation

"In some situations, a team of speakers, not just one person, is a normal expectation."

Although Grace could do a good job presenting on her own, there may be other situations in which a team working together on the platform will communicate more powerfully.

Close collaboration

"If I am working closely with members of a small group and sharing responsibilities with them, then a presentation concerning our project will be more powerful if we present as a team. The speakers can support each other."

Unspoken message

"On some occasions, the presence of a team of presenters delivers a powerful, unspoken message to the audience about the unity of the group."

When you are considering whether a team presentation is the correct choice, the expressed wish or expectation of the audience should be the decisive factor: If it suits the audience, make a team presentation.

Most of the time, if a team presentation suits the audience, then it will be the stronger, more effective option as well. In other words, the two reasons generally coincide.

Conrad works for Maxibuild as the site director for a large construction project. A few days ago, he made a presentation to the client along with the four managers on his project team. He is talking to Randal about the presentation, and it is clear that a team presentation was the right choice: It was right for the client and it made the presentation stronger.

Audience request

"I spoke to the client's CEO, and he wanted all of us to be there to explain why-- from our individual points of view--the project is a month behind schedule."

Audience expectation

"Even if the CEO hadn't requested it, I would have included the whole team in the presentation. I knew that as we were examining the status of the entire project, he would have expected each discipline to have a spokesperson."

Close collaboration

"Because I work closely with the other managers on a daily basis, I felt we needed to be in the same room together, supporting each other, for this important presentation."

Unspoken message

"I'm leading a strong team, and we are all pulling together to make up for lost time. That's the message that we delivered by presenting together in the same room."

Question

You are listening to colleagues discussing the circumstances under which they would expect to make a team presentation rather than work on their own. Which circumstances indicate that a team presentation is the correct choice?

Options:

1. "If I am part of a project team, working closely with others, we would present as a team."
2. "If the clients say that they want to hear from several people, then we present as a team."
3. "If it would be more enjoyable for us to present as a team, we would do so."
4. "If the audience expects a team presentation in that situation, then we present as a team."
5. "If the audience will ask a lot of questions, we present as a team."
6. "If presenting as a group would deliver a strong, unspoken message about unity, we would present together."

Answer:

You would expect to make a team presentation if you are part of a project team, if the group could deliver a silent message about unity, if a team presentation is normal in the situation, or if it has been requested by the audience.

Option 1: This is a correct choice. The members of the team can support each other if they present as a team. If the work is already collaborative, it may make sense for your colleagues to present as a team as well.

Option 2: This is a correct choice. Sometimes a client will specify that they expect to hear from multiple people.

Giving Successful Presentations

In those instances, your colleagues should make a team presentation and include the people that are expected by the audience.

Option 3: This is an incorrect choice. Your colleagues should not present as a team just because they enjoy it. They should have good reason for doing so, like a client request, the work was done as a team, or to send a message of unity.

Option 4: This choice is correct. An audience may expect to see multiple people presenting together on a topic. If that's the case, your colleagues should present as a team. This expectation may be explicit or assumed.

Option 5: This choice is incorrect. The number of questions expected does not dictate whether to present as a team. Make the decision based on factors like client requests, audience expectations, or a need to show a unified team.

Option 6: This choice is correct. There are times when your colleagues will need to demonstrate that multiple players are unified on a topic. By presenting as a team, they send the message that they're working as a team.

Make a team presentation when it will add to the strength of the presentation or meet an expectation of the audience.

PREPARING FOR A TEAM PRESENTATION

Preparing for a team presentation

You can't prepare for a team presentation the same way you would if you were presenting alone. Like any other situation in which you're working closely with a group of other people, you need to coordinate your efforts.

Jorge is giving a presentation with three colleagues in a couple of weeks. He calls Marie, one of the colleagues, to discuss the upcoming presentation.

Jorge: Marie, the four of us need to get together and prepare our team presentation.

Marie: You're right. We might need more than one meeting, in fact. Jorge: That's quite possible. How about Monday afternoon?

Marie: That's fine.

Jorge: Good. I'll contact Vicki and Kevin. And meanwhile, we can exchange some e- mails or talk again on the phone about aspects of the preparation.

Giving Successful Presentations

The first requirements of team preparation are that the presenters:
- contact each other well in advance of the presentation,
- meet face-to-face as often as necessary.

Question

You expect to prepare several team presentations over the next month. You list the basic requirements of the preparation process. Which requirements do you include on your list?

Options:

1. I can rely on e-mail and telephone contact with the other team members.

2. I must establish contact with the other presenters well before the presentation date.

3. We need to meet face to face, as often as necessary.

4. We need to meet once, as close to the date of the presentation as possible.

5. We need to prepare independently until the day before the presentation.

Answer:

In fact, you need to make contact with the rest of the team well before the presentation and meet as often as necessary.

Option 1: This choice is incorrect. While you can use e-mail and telephone contact, this should not be the only way your team prepares. You and your team should have as many face-to-face meetings as necessary.

Option 2: This choice is correct. Contact the other presenters well in advance of the presentation so you can arrange meetings when everyone can work together, and so there will be enough time to schedule all the necessary meetings.

Option 3: This is a correct choice. Some of the discussions can be handled by e-mail and telephone. However, your team needs to meet face-to-face to prepare effectively for the presentation. Schedule face to face meetings as often as necessary.

Option 4: This is an incorrect choice. The team should meet as many times as necessary for adequate preparation. Contact your team members well in advance to make proper arrangements for scheduling a meeting.

Option 5: This choice is incorrect. The team members need to meet multiple times and start well in advance of the presentation date. The team needs to meet face-to-face as often as necessary and work together on the presentation.

You maintain a dialog with your fellow team members through telephone calls, e-mail and--most importantly--meeting with them. What is the objective of that dialog?

There are several vital matters that Jorge and the rest of his team need to discuss as they prepare their presentation.

Content

"We have to agree on exactly what content will be covered, so that we sound like a team. We may have different or overlapping ideas at the start of the preparation process."

Appearance

"We need to determine which elements of our physical appearance to coordinate so that we look like a team."

Actions

Giving Successful Presentations

"We need to discuss and decide how to organize ourselves as a team in the presentation room."

Team presentations are usually inadequately prepared. The team members prepare their individual contributions independently instead of working together on those elements of the presentation that will make them appear to be a cohesive team--or not. To come across as a team, you must coordinate your presentation content, physical appearance, and plans for the presentation venue.

Question

One of your colleagues is preparing a team presentation. She is planning an active dialog with her fellow team members to coordinate the presentation. She asks you what they should discuss and decide on. What do you say?

Options:

1. "You should decide what color suit you all need to wear to present a similar appearance to the audience."

2. "Decide how, and to what extent, you will project a similar physical appearance."

3. "You have to decide how you will organize yourselves in the presentation room in order for the audience to have a good view."

4. "You must agree on what the presentation will cover, and how it will do so."

5. "You have to decide how you will arrange yourselves as a team in the presentation venue."

Answer:

You need to determine what content you will cover and how, the elements of your physical appearance that you will coordinate, and how to arrange yourselves as a team in the presentation room.

Option 1: Incorrect. Appearance does need to be coordinated, but not to the level of the color of clothing. The team can coordinate how formal their dress will be and any branding they might wear, such as badges or name tags.

Option 2: This is a correct choice. Your colleague's team should discuss how they want to coordinate their appearance. This would include how formally everyone will dress and whether everyone will wear name badges or tags.

Option 3: This choice is incorrect. Your colleague's team should discuss how they will sit during the presentation, but not for reasons of audience visibility. Her team should discuss what physical arrangement is best for their presentation.

Option 4: This choice is correct. The team members should discuss what will be covered and how. Each team member should voice what content they think needs to be included, and then the team needs to agree on what will actually be covered.

Option 5: This is a correct choice. It is necessary for the team to determine just how people will sit and who will chair the presentation. The chair should sit in the center, and the others should be arranged around that person.

Barbara, a manager at Ace Apparel, often gives presentations with her team to both internal and external audiences. As a professional, Barbara insists on meticulous attention to the preparation details.

What decisions about content, appearance, and team arrangement does she make at the preparation stage?

Presentation content

"We share the content among the team members. We always know what area of content each speaker is responsible for--that way we cover all the necessary content. Each of us repeats important messages for reinforcement."

Physical appearance

"We agree on a dress code that suits the occasion and decide whether we will wear badges or any other form of branding."

Team organization

"Part of preparing is agreeing on where everyone will sit during the presentation and who will chair the presentation. The chairperson sits in the middle."

Content is normally divided on the basis of expertise or responsibility; you wouldn't agree to a situation in which one person makes a presentation, and the others only answer questions. If everyone repeats one or two key messages, amplifying them in his own way, this communicates that you are working as a team. A dress code does not mean that you wear a uniform. But you will not look like a team if one person wears clothes that clearly clash with the rest of the team's clothes.

You also won't look like a team if one person is wearing a badge but the others are not. For an external presentation, branding might mean everyone having a folder with the company logo, but for an internal presentation, this kind of branding is not important.

Conservative business dress is a sound choice for a presentation to management, and there is no reason to wear badges for an internal presentation.

Case Study: Question 1 of 3
Scenario

You work for Lux Interiors. With a group of four colleagues, you'll manage the remodeling of locations in the Oak Hotels group. The management of Oak Hotels has requested a presentation about the project from the project management team. You are having a meeting with your colleagues to discuss this team presentation.

Answer the following questions, in order, to show how you will prepare for the presentation.

Question

The first thing you discuss with your four colleagues is the presentation content. Carol thinks that you, as the most senior person on the project, should decide what needs to be said and make a presentation on behalf of the team. Everyone else should be there only to answer questions at the end. What do you say?

Options:

1. "I'll decide on the overall content and the messages to repeat--such as the need for low disruption during the remodeling. But we should each speak about our own area of responsibility."

2. "I agree. I'll decide that content and prepare a presentation. The rest of you can just handle questions in your areas of expertise."

3. "I don't agree. We should all decide what needs to be said and what messages to repeat. Then I will know that my presentation represents the team."

4. "We should agree on the content together, and each of us should make a presentation about the hotels we deal with. But we should all reiterate our commitment to low disruption during remodeling."

Answer:

Giving Successful Presentations

You must decide on the presentation content at the preparation stage. You then divide it among the speakers and agree what messages need to be repeated by all.

Option 1: This choice is incorrect. The team should decide together what content is to be covered. Each presenter will emphasize important points and cover their area of expertise. However, the whole group is responsible for content decisions.

Option 2: This is an incorrect choice. The team should decide on the content together, and all of the team members should present based on their area of expertise. Everyone should present equally and answer questions equally.

Option 3: This choice is incorrect. Everyone does need to agree on what will be covered. However, everyone should also be involved in the presentation; you are not the only one presenting. The team should also agree on who presents which parts.

Option 4: This is the correct choice. This response focuses on the team deciding as a group what will be covered. It also emphasizes that everyone will present the parts for their area of expertise and what important messages everyone will repeat.

Case Study: Question 2 of 3

You discuss with your colleagues how to coordinate the physical appearance of team members during the presentation. What do you decide?

Options:

1. Normal business attire is the right way to dress for the occasion.
2. We should wear whatever we want.
3. We should wear name badges.

4. One or two of us could carry a Lux Interiors brochure with our notes.

Answer:

You must agree on a dress code. You also have to decide whether the team members should wear name badges or any other form of branding.

Option 1: This is a correct choice. Conservative business attire is always an appropriate choice. Your team should have a unified, professional appearance, which means everyone looks like a business professional.

Option 2: This is an incorrect choice. While team members can choose what they will wear, the choices are not unlimited. The team decided they should all wear conservative business attire for a unified, professional appearance.

Option 3: This is a correct choice. Since your team will be presenting to an external audience, name badges are a good idea. Members of the Oak Hotels management team probably will not know everyone on your team, so name tags will be helpful.

Option 4: This choice is incorrect. A couple of people carrying company brochures will not be helpful in identifying your team members. Instead, team members should each wear a name badge showing the company branding and their name.

Case Study: Question 3 of 3

With the rest of the team, you discuss your team organization in the presentation room. What do you suggest?

Options:

Giving Successful Presentations

1. "We need to decide where we'll sit. If I'm going to chair the presentation, I'd like to sit on the end of the row."

2. "I will chair the meeting, if nobody objects. I'll sit in the middle, with two of you on either side."

3. "When we arrive at the venue, we should decide about seating and a chairperson for the presentation."

Answer:

In fact, you have to choose someone to chair the presentation, and you need to decide on the seating arrangement. The chairperson is always in the middle.

Option 1: This is an incorrect choice. The chair should not sit at the end of the row. Instead, the chair should sit in the middle. The team should decide where everyone is going to sit prior to arriving at the venue.

Option 2: This is the correct choice. While it makes sense for you to chair the meeting, make sure everyone else agrees. The chair will sit in the middle of the group, and the team should decide where everyone else sits.

Option 3: This is an incorrect choice. The seating arrangement should be decided prior to arriving at the venue. Since you will be chairing the session, you sit in the middle, and the team decides in advance where everyone else will sit.

Having the team members discuss the hotels they are responsible for is a good way to divide the content, and repeating the message about minimum disruption will reinforce the idea that this is a team effort. Your decisions about dress code and name badges mean that you will present a coordinated appearance. Determining the seating arrangement and who should chair the meeting will convey that you are organized as a team. All of these things should be decided at the preparation stage.

A successful team presentation requires preparation that coordinates content, physical appearance, and team organization.

DETERMINING TO WHAT EXTENT THE SPEAKERS BEHAVE AS A TEAM

Determining to what extent the speakers behave as a team

You are part of a team presentation. One of your colleagues is speaking to the audience. What should you be doing? Delivering a convincing team presentation requires each team member to act as though he really is part of a team--throughout the entire presentation.

William is thinking about a team presentation he saw yesterday in which the team members behaved as individuals.

While the first person was presenting, it seemed to me that everybody else tuned out; they were probably thinking about their own speeches.

They certainly weren't behaving in a way that supported the speaker.

Of book, you need to rehearse how you'll support the speaker--I think these people hadn't rehearsed their presentation even once.

Delivering a convincing team presentation requires that the team members behave in ways that support each other. The presentation delivery must be rehearsed so that these supportive behaviors are practiced.

Question

You have prepared your team presentation with your colleagues. Now you make a list of the keys to delivering the presentation convincingly, as a team. Which suggestions have you included on your list?

Options:

1. Each of us must concentrate on delivering our own speech really well.

2. While the presentation is being delivered, we need to behave in ways that support each other.

3. While one of our colleagues is talking, we should take the opportunity to think about our own speeches.

4. We need to rehearse the presentation to practice supportive behaviors.

5. Each speaker should deliver his portion of the presentation with spontaneity.

Answer:

In fact, delivering a presentation convincingly as a team requires that team member behave in ways that support colleagues. These behaviors need to be rehearsed.

Option 1: This is an incorrect choice. If everyone concentrates on only their part, they won't behave like a team, just as a set of individuals. Instead, the team should practice supportive behaviors and display those during the presentation.

Option 2: This choice is correct. Your team should show support for each other while each person is presenting.

Giving Successful Presentations

You should not look like you're bored or preparing for your own part. Instead, you should listen to each other and act engaged.

Option 3: This choice is incorrect. While one of your other colleagues is talking, you listen to that person. If you study your own speeches, the audience will notice and think you don't look like a team.

Option 4: This is a correct choice. A convincing team presentation requires that the team looks like they support one another. To make this convincing, practice supporting behaviors prior to the presentation.

Option 5: This is an incorrect choice. Delivering with spontaneity will not help your group look like a team. To deliver a team presentation convincingly, practice supportive behavior, and show your support for each other during the delivery.

What should you do to show that the presentation is genuinely a group effort, not simply a series of unconnected solo speeches?

There are three basic ways in which team members should help each other while the presentation is being delivered.

Support 1

While one person is speaking, the others can provide support by listening all the time.

Support 2

While one person is speaking, the other team members must provide support by responding appropriately.

Support 3

The team member who is chairing the presentation should be active in her role in relation to other members of the team. This is an important support mechanism.

It is not difficult to contribute actively to the presentation, even when you are not speaking. But remember, there is an enormous distraction that must be resisted: the temptation to think about your own speech.

The supportive role of the chairperson, introducing and thanking the other speakers, must be distinguished from the other duties of the chair--for example, summarizing at the end and thanking the audience for its attention.

Question

You will soon make your first team presentation. Unfortunately, your fellow presenters do not know how to support each other as the presentation is being delivered. What do you say to them?

Options:

1. "The person who chairs the presentation needs to be active in supporting her colleagues."

2. "While one person is speaking, the rest of us should listen the whole time."

3. "We should all be willing to answer any question from the audience."

4. "We need to react appropriately to the speaker."

5. "As one person is speaking, the rest of us must avoid reacting in a noticeable way."

Answer:

Actually, supportive behavior requires everyone to listen and respond appropriately to the speaker, while the person chairing the presentation should exert active control.

Option 1: This is a correct choice. The chair of the presentation is an important support position. The chair introduces the presentation and the speakers and summarizes at the end. He or she can facilitate good support for the presenters.

Option 2: This choice is correct. Show support for each other by listening during each presentation. Not listening will distract the audience, but listening shows you care about what the other team members are saying.

Option 3: This is an incorrect choice. While you should be willing to answer questions, this does not necessarily show support for the team. The way to show support for each other during the presentation, is by listening when others are speaking.

Option 4: This is a correct choice. Reactions may include nodding in agreement or laughing at appropriate moments. If you do not respond to what is being said, the audience will think you're not listening, which detracts from the image of support.

Option 5: This is an incorrect choice. To the contrary, you should react appropriately to the others' presentations. You can nod your head or even laugh if they make a joke. These actions show you are listening and support the speaker.

William was privileged to attend a great team presentation a few days ago. Four people from marketing spoke about a campaign they'd been working on. William was really impressed by the ways in which they all supported each other.

Listening

"The team members who weren't speaking looked at the speaker while she spoke; they also inclined their bodies in the direction of the speaker. It was clear that they were listening."

Responding

"They reacted to what the speaker was saying. If it was something really important or something they agreed with, they nodded. If it was something amusing, some of them smiled or laughed."

Controlling

"The woman who chaired the presentation actively controlled the occasion. She introduced the speakers at the beginning, introduced each of the speakers when it was their turn, and then thanked them when they finished."

To listen actively, turn toward the speaker, at least partially, and lean forward--at least a little. If you are genuinely listening to the speaker, then you will naturally respond with supportive facial or vocal gestures. Your face will look animated, rather than vacant.

The chairperson will introduce each speaker in turn by saying something like, "Now we're going to hear from X who's going to talk about Y."

It is important that you behave as a team by supporting the speaker in ways that look natural. Looking at the speaker means generally looking at him or her, not staring the whole time. Responding to the speaker does not mean that the team members should laugh at every joke or nod at everything they agree with.

Although you will have rehearsed the delivery of your team presentation, it is vital that the way you listen and respond does not appear rehearsed or staged.

Now decide how successful the speakers are at delivering their presentation as a team in the example that follows.

Paula has just attended a sales presentation given by a small sales team from Advanced Scanners, which hopes to make a sale to her hospital. The salespeople emphasized that, in addition to the technological excellence of their scanners, clients benefited from the fact that a dedicated support team was available.

Eye contact

"A number of times, I noticed one of the speakers catch the eye of a colleague who was turned in her direction as she was making a point."

Nodding

"While the first team member was talking about the ease of use of the scanner, his colleagues were nodding their heads in his direction, so they clearly think that ease of use is a major advantage."

Introducing

"The chairperson introduced us to the rest of the team at the beginning. Then she invited each speaker in turn to talk and then thanked them for their contributions."

Natural behavior

"The last team presentation I saw was very efficient, but watching the way they reacted to each other was a bit like watching a group of actors at work. The Advanced Scanners people were more natural-looking, and comfortable with each other."

From Paula's description, the Advanced Scanner people did an excellent job of behaving as a team. Speakers were able to make eye contact with non-speakers, who were turned toward them, and non-speakers nodded their approval when a point was made about an important benefit of the scanner. Also, the person chairing the presentation exerted active control through her introductions and her expressions of thanks.

The supportive behavior of the team members was apparent but, at the same time, it did not appear to be false.

In a couple of important ways, the Foodall managers deliver their presentation as a team. They listen and respond, and they do so in ways that do not seem false or theatrical: Joan believes in their expressions of enthusiasm about the future. Unfortunately, although the factory manager who is chairing the occasion is active in his relationship with the audience, he is not active in relation to his colleagues: He does not exert team control.

Delivering an effective team presentation requires you to demonstrate to the audience that you are a team by how each team member listens and responds to his colleagues, and through the active role of the chairperson.

REFERENCES

References
1. **Making Successful Presentations** - 1995, Forsyth, Patrick, Sheldon Press
2. **Making Presentations** - 1998, Hindle, Tim, Dorling Kindersley
3. **Voice and the Actor** - 1989, Berry, Cicely
4. **Creating Presentations** - 2000, Burrows, Terry, Dorling Kindersley

GLOSSARY

Glossary

A

audience - The group of people to whom the presentation is being made. The relationship between a presenter and an audience is not normally a passive one; the audience is encouraged to interact.

C

content - The ideas and information contained in the presentation, and which is normally structured hierarchically into main points and supporting sub-points.

I

interactivity - Reaction by the audience, and encouraged by the presenter, in the book of his or her presentation, and perhaps including the asking of questions, group work and the handling of objects.

M

message - The key information or idea that the presenter wants the audience to remember and act on and which provides the key focus of his or her efforts to communicate during the presentation.

P

presentation - An occasion at which a speaker introduces ideas and/or information to a listening audience in a pre-prepared form. The speaker may use technological support, for example slides, and usually allows or encourages questions from the audience at some point.

presentation environment - The physical circumstances under which the presentation is made and which influence its likely success. The most important elements of the environment are the size and shape of the venue, the equipment and the configuration of seating.

presentation objective - The purpose for which a presenter makes a presentation, in other words how he or she wants to change or influence the audience as a result of the presentation.

presenter - A person who gives a presentation.

R

rehearsal - An activity in which the speaker familiarizes him or herself with the words and actions of a presentation by simulating them, sometimes wholly, sometimes in part.

www.ingramcontent.com/pod-product-compliance
Lightning Source LLC
Chambersburg PA
CBHW021546200526
45163CB00016B/2515